MODERN DAY SLAVERY AND WHAT WE BUY

I0448853

HEARING

BEFORE THE

TOM LANTOS HUMAN RIGHTS COMMISSION

HOUSE OF REPRESENTATIVES

ONE HUNDRED AND FOURTEENTH CONGRESS

SECOND SESSION

JULY 24, 2014

Available via the World Wide Web: http://www.tlhrc.house.gov

CONTENTS

WITNESSES

LETTERS, STATEMENTS, ETC., SUBMITTED FOR THE HEARING

APPENDIX

MODERN DAY SLAVERY AND WHAT WE BUY

THURSDAY, JULY 24, 2014

House of Representatives,
Tom Lantos Human Rights Commission,
Washington, D.C.

The commission met, pursuant to call, at 10:00 a.m., in Room 2255 Rayburn House Office Building, Hon. Suzanne Bonamici, [Executive Committee Member of the Commission] presiding.

Ms. BONAMICI. Good morning. I want to thank everyone for being here today at the Tom Lantos Human Rights Commission hearing on international human trafficking and forced labor.

In particular, I want to thank the staff of the Tom Lantos Human Rights Commission for coordinating this hearing and our witnesses for their leadership in combating modern-day slavery.

I welcome our distinguished panelists including from the administration and representatives from the nongovernmental human rights and humanitarian communities. I look forward to hearing from them about the diplomatic and humanitarian measures needed to address this crisis.

That in the 21st century more than 20 million people worldwide find themselves living in conditions of modern-day slavery is an affront to humanity and our basic liberties enshrined in the Universal Declaration of Human Rights.

According to the International Labor Organization's 2012 findings, 22 percent are victims of forced sexual exploitation with 68 percent victims of forced labor.

These men, women and children are unconscionably subjugated to conditions of slavery for the sake of a profit. According to a new ILO report, trafficking generates $150 billion in illegal profits each year. Of this, two-thirds is generated from sexual exploitation with approximately $51 billion generated as a result of forced labor.

Trafficking for the purpose of sexual exploitation as historically been the most commonly reported and prosecuted form of human trafficking globally. However, in our globalized economy with increasing demands for cheap migrant labor worldwide labor trafficking has become an insidious growth industry as it is inadequately regulated and it preys on the vulnerable.

Victims of forced labor and debt bondage are held in conditions of slavery in a variety of jobs including agricultural and construction work, domestic servitude and other labor intensive jobs.

Vulnerable men, women and children trying to provide for their families are often the targets of exploitation in trafficking as a means to minimize overhead costs and provide cheaper goods at market.

The spreading of forced labor has therefore led to an increase in its effects on the production, handling and distribution of various goods. By now we have all heard stories of shoppers finding desperate cries for help in the forms of notes stuffed into bags or stitched into clothing tags exported from factories worldwide to shops in our local neighborhoods.

More recently, we have heard about harsh conditions endured by migrants and refugees forcibly employed in the fishing trade in Thailand. If we are to root out this horrific scourge on humanity we must have a multi-faceted approach to combat the root problems of the crisis and to hold accountable governments of countries that are sources, destinations or transit centers for the innocent victims of trafficking and forced labor.

I want to express my appreciation to Secretary of State John Kerry and Ambassador Luis CdeBaca and the staff of his office for their conviction and commitment to addressing these human rights violations and paving the road from victim to survivor as expressed in a newly released 2014 Trafficking in Persons report.

Though we have truly made progress, I expect Ambassador CdeBaca will be the first to agree that there is still much more to do before we can live in a world rid of slavery and exploitation.

Congress must ensure that we work harder to eradicate this egregious human rights violation. To that end, on June 11th, Representatives Maloney and Smith introduced H.R. 4842, the Business Supply Chain Transparency on Trafficking and Slavery Act of 2014.

This legislation seeks to require certain companies to disclose information describing any measures the company has taken to identify and address conditions of forced labor, slavery, human trafficking and the worst forms of child labor within the companies' supply chains.

However, as this is a global problem, so too the solution must be global. The U.S. government must play a role in supporting global initiatives such as the ILO protocol of 2014 to the Forced Labor Convention, 1930 and ILO Convention on Decent Work for Domestic Workers.

Today's hearing will examine current trends in human trafficking and forced labor across the globe. I hope, in addition to outlining shortcomings in the battle on human trafficking it will also highlight key successes and initiatives.

It is now time to hear from our first witness. Ambassador Luis CdeBaca directs the State Department's Office of Monitor and Combat Trafficking in Persons, which advocates for an end to modern slavery.

And then we will have a second panel with many very qualified witnesses. And I also want to submit into the record any oral testimony along with the written testimony already provided by the witnesses.

Ambassador.

STATEMENT OF AMBASSADOR LUIS CDEBACA, AMBASSADOR-AT-LARGE, OFFICE TO MONITOR AND COMBAT TRAFFICKING IN PERSONS, DEPARTMENT OF STATE

AMABSSADOR CdeBACA. Thank you, Representative, and members of the commission entirely. Tom Lantos was a leading light in getting the Trafficking Victims Protection bill passed and was such an example to so many of us whether we worked on his committee or were staff on sister committees and for me being able to appear before the commission is personally very gratifying because of what he meant to me when I was working at Judiciary.

But I want to talk first about somebody who means a lot to us in the trafficking office and that is Frederick Douglass, one of the first African-American ambassadors that the United States ever had but, more importantly, a person who escaped slavery and worked so hard to eradicate it, not just for his own community -- African-American community -- but around the United States and around the world.

He said one time that, "I prayed for my freedom for 20 years and never got an answer until I prayed with my feet," and that notion of the journey to freedom being something that is not ours to give to the victims but rather a journey to walk with them on and really think of them as survivors -- people who can pray with their feet and can get out.

And so one of the things that I want to just highlight in my testimony today is that notion of the survivors as being full participants in this fight. This isn't something we are doing for them or something we are doing to them but, rather, we are doing with them.

As you mentioned, Secretary Kerry released the annual Trafficking in Persons about a month ago and it looks at the ongoing challenges of fighting human trafficking in about 190 countries and territories around the world.

We have come a long way in our shared fight and we saw and we are very happy with the fact that about 45,000 victims were identified by governments in the last year. But up against the International Labor Organization's most recent estimate -- a conservative one -- suggesting that there are over 21 million trafficking victims in the world -- people held in servitude even as we speak, clearly, we have a lot more work to do.

First, the diagnostics -- as you know, trafficking in persons covers all the activities involving holding a person in a condition of compelled service. Despite the name, it doesn't require moving a victim. Indeed, many people in forced labor around the world work in or near their home communities.

But it does require the use of force, fraud or coercion to compel or maintain someone in labor or sexual exploitation unless, of course, they are under 18, for commercial sex.

Each year we look at government efforts around the world through this 3-P paradigm of prevention, protection and prosecution. I grew up on a farm so, of course, I have to make a agricultural reference. It is the three legs of the milking stool. You fall over if you only have two legs or even one.

Prevention, protection and prosecution all together, and the TIP report ranks these countries. Last year, 31 governments in Tier I, which is not getting an A on the test -- this is basically the equivalent of a C -- meeting the minimum standards.

The United States is one of those and we are doing some interesting things. We have got 55 of the 57 states and territories have passed modern anti-trafficking legislation and every year we see more and more good policies, good training, more and more good outcomes for trafficking victims and yet all I can say about the United States is that we are meeting the minimum standards.

I would like to say that the United States and the other 31 counties on Tier I are doing well and we are going to keep working to make sure that we can get to that point. But right now we are talking about doing the bare minimum.

Eighty-nine governments in Tier II -- 44 on the Tier II watch list and then 23 governments on the lowest level, which is Tier III. A couple of progress stars this year that I would like to point out, Chile and Switzerland, both moved up into Tier I of the report in part thanks to President Obama's meeting with former President Pinera in March of 2011 and the ongoing commitment of President Bachelet since she has come back.

Chilean authorities have strengthened anti-trafficking law enforcement efforts to rebuilding police and prosecutor capacity. They obtained their first convictions for labor trafficking, increased inter-agency coordination and created a national action plan and victim assistance protocol -- all of the things that we have seen as a recipe for success around the world.

In Switzerland, the government passed a law prohibiting the prostitution of minors for the first time, convicted more traffickers, issued more serious prison sentences and launched the first ever nationwide awareness campaign.

It has taken a lot of time and dedication both from the United States and Switzerland to get to that point including the personal commitment of our ambassadors, Don Beyer and Suzi LeVine, which is much appreciated.

We have seen a number of other countries where we have had progress and it is put forward in my written testimony but I do want to call out one here in the hemisphere and that is Haiti.

Amazingly, in a country where a slave revolt led to the creation of a new nation, Haiti had never made slavery a criminal offense and paid for it with almost 300,000 children in domestic servitude in the practice known as restavek that really is a form of modern slavery.

Two hundred and ten years after slaves seized their own freedom, the passage of the Modern Anti-Trafficking legislation this spring made modern slavery illegal in Haiti and it was very welcomed.

We also this year in the report saw the operation of the auto-downgrade provision of the 2008 law, which basically said that countries can only be on Tier II watch list for X number of years before they automatically have to fall down to Tier III. If they are just stagnant they are actually moving backwards.

It might be the jet lag talking from the trip that I was on last week but, you know, it is like being on one of the moving walkways at the airport. If you are just standing there facing the wrong direction, you are moving backwards.

So the auto-downgrade provision really was looking at how do you incentivize governments to move and we saw that with Afghanistan, Barbados, Chad and the Maldives -- countries that took action, made serious efforts and did not get subjected to that automatic downgrade provision in the law.

But two significant allies and important trade partners of the United States did not show significant improvement. Thailand and Malaysia were put on Tier III this year as a result of that auto-downgrade provision and their lack of sufficient progress going forward.

Over the coming years, things to look at both in you and your oversight function and us in our diplomacy will be the four countries that face the automatic downgrade next year -- Angola, Belarus, Burundi and the Comoros.

While human trafficking may seem far away, in reality it is very much a part of our daily lives. Not only does it happen here in the United States in both urban and rural settings -- over 350 calls to the national hotline from Oregon alone last year -- but in a globalized world goods and services tainted from forced labor can easily enter the closets, pantries and garages of even the most dedicated modern abolitionists.

We continue to see, in the report this year, widespread use of forced labor throughout the world in a wide range of industries and while governments have typically had more success in identifying and responding to sex trafficking cases than labor trafficking and we do not want anyone to back off of those efforts, more must be done to combat all forms of modern slavery.

A couple of sectors that I want to point out -- forced labor in mining was noted in 46 of the debt narratives this year but the actions do not match the exploitation. No prosecutions or convictions whatsoever in the mining sector.

And we are talking not the Klondike Gold Rush here. We are talking about artisanal mining -- people scraping tantalum and coltan and other things that come into our cellphones, come into our mobile technologies, all the way from the Eastern Congo and other places.

Highlighting the interconnections between human trafficking forms, sex trafficking related to the mining industry is discussed in 15 of the narratives -- 15 countries where we saw that happening.

Now, there were some prosecutions for -- in Senegal and Namibia and one conviction in Senegal. We have a long way to go to tell consumers that the mineral they use, whether it is the mica that makes the lipstick glittery or whether it is the coltan that makes your cellphone not burn your pocket is somehow slavery-free.

Forced labor in agriculture is also very prevalent and it is discussed in 126 narratives -- 67 percent of the countries covered in the report we saw forced labor in agriculture including the United States. The report describes forced labor in activities as diverse as cattle herding and cultivating coca, tea, potatoes, bananas, palm oil, sugar cane and coffee.

I have had many of those things in the last week and I can't tell you whether or not they came from a place that was exploitation free, despite the fact of what I do for a living.

Forced labor in the seafood sector is discussed in 51 narratives with four prosecutions and two convictions recorded and, again, the demand for commercial sex act related to the fishery sector exists and it is noted in eight countries around the world.

So what are we doing in the face of these facts? We are supporting programs to counter forced labor in supply chains such as work being done by the Solidarity Center in Bangkok to address human trafficking and other labor issues in the migrant communities.

We are funding projects with the ILO and the U.N. Office of Drugs and Crime that address the role of recruitment fees charged to employees in facilitating human trafficking.

The final ILO global report will be based on field research in Vietnam, China, and Paraguay and the UNODC global report will focus on a criminal justice response and its impact in UAE, Thailand and Mexico.

Congressman, you mentioned the ILO report -- 150 billion reasons why we have to fight human trafficking telling us that this is not just a moral issue. This is not just a security issue. This is also an economic issue -- $150 billion industry around the world.

The conclusion of the ILO report is undeniable and I will simply quote them. "The continued existence of forced labor is bad for business, bad for development and bad for its victims. It is a practice that has no place in modern society and should be eradicated as soon as possible."

A couple of very quick things that we are doing to address trafficking in the supply chain most important to ensure that our tax dollars don't support this crime, President Obama signed an executive order two years ago strengthening protections against human trafficking in federal contracts and were happy to say that the regulations carrying out that order are in their final stages.

We have had good input from NGOs, from the business community, from the academy to really look at that

and one thing that I am struck by is the shared commitment and the shared values of all of the different actors to ensure that we have a slavery-free supply chain.

As the largest purchaser of goods in the global economy this was an important step that both signals to U.S. corporations what is expected by the largest customer in the world but also demonstrates an approach that other governments can take to strengthen protections in their own procurement.

I would like to take a few moments to discuss the victims of this crime as well. The thematic focus, as you mentioned, Congresswoman, is the journey from victim to survivor.

The impact of human trafficking is horrifying. Those who escape modern slavery struggle to recover, heal, reclaim their lives. It is not an easy path and true recovery is far from guaranteed but it can happen and governments can hasten that process.

But the report also highlights the importance of empowering trafficking survivors to strengthen the anti-trafficking movement itself and as Secretary Kerry explains -- and we know this from the domestic violence work, we know this from the sexual violence movement over the last 25 of 30 years -- from their experiences survivors know better than anyone else the types of protections and opportunities that would help ensure others don't go through the same thing.

Someone who was invisible to police can provide advice on what law enforcement should have looked for, what types of awareness campaigns might have helped him or her see that they were a victim of a crime.

A survivor who cooperated in the conviction of their trafficker knows best what made her participation in that process less traumatic and more effective.

Survivors are strong. They are perhaps our best hope and our most overlooked resource for ending modern slavery once and for all. This was brought home to me in a vivid way yesterday when we hosted our annual intern roundtable which brought over 350 interns from across town to think about this journey.

There, we saw survivor caucus member Evelyn Chumbow and special assistant to the president Amy Pope sharing a podium. A decade ago, the newly liberated child slave Evelyn met for the first time the young prosecutor Amy Pope and that day made the hard choice to trust her, to put her story forward and to take that leap that somebody from the government would actually help her pursue justice.

A decade later yesterday we saw the two of them together again as colleagues, confronting modern slavery together but as equals. And that is what we are fighting for when we talk about this journey to freedom.

So, finally, what is the way forward? The TIP report and the tier rankings are a means to an end, not an end to themselves. We must not lose sight of the true goal, which is stopping modern slavery and helping victims recover.

Only with concrete programs to help them find their voice and reclaim their lives can we help them become survivors. Recent years have seen increased concerned about the stewardship of natural resources, ethical treatment of animals and ensuring that farmers receive fair prices for their work.

As a result, certifications and labels exist to inform customers whether seafood is sustainable caught, livestock is pasture fed, chickens are free range, coffee beans are fair trade, diamonds are conflict free -- I could go on and on.

And yet those seals of approval, while fostering increased transparency and driving consumers to reward companies that engage in good corporate citizenship they all seem to assume that the hands that pull the net, that the hands that pick the crops are not enslaved.

We know that that assumption is nonoperative. We have a responsibility to the 20 plus million people around the world to break that cycle of human trafficking that forms the base of so many products and goods, to drive out of supply chains the patterns of vulnerabilities to forced labor and to address the socioeconomic foundations of poverty that ensnare so many into these exploitative situations.

It will continue to require leaders throughout society -- community workers, activists, faith groups, organized labor, government officials, industry leaders -- to encourage producers to monitor their supply chains and buy and sell goods and services free of forced labor.

So we will continue to build our knowledge of forced labor in the supply. We will continue to expand our collaboration with other governments, the corporate sector and civil society and we look forward to working with you and Congress to proclaim freedom and seek justice so that we can achieve our ultimate goal -- a world without slavery.

[The written statement of Ambassador CdeBaca is not available]

Ms. BONAMICI. Thank you very much, Ambassador. That was excellent testimony. We are fortunate to have you as the ambassador. I know when you talked about the three-pronged approach -- prevention, protection and prosecution -- that you as a former prosecutor really understand the importance of enforcement.

It isn't just having the policies in effect. It is the enforcement that goes with them as well that is so important. I wanted to ask you a little bit about the TIP -- the Trafficking in Persons report.

It is my understanding that the U.S. just became included in the rankings in 2010 so can you talk a little bit about the -- how that happened? What are the advantages to having the United States as a listed country and has this encouraged other countries to improve their own ratings and rankings?

I know you talked about the slipping back and being downgraded. But has there been some indication that there have been more encouragement for other countries as the U.S. serving as a model to other countries to improve their records?

AMABSSADOR CdeBACA. One of the things that in the decision to include the United States in the report that Secretary Clinton and I talked a lot about was this notion of would people discount it automatically by saying oh, of course, you are going to give yourself a great ranking on your own report.

And at the end of the day, we felt that the risks of that were far outweighed by the salutary effect of putting it on. It has done a couple of things, I think. First of all, the rigor of the minimum standards analysis that we do for all of the other countries of the world is something that has helped us in the United States.

We do this through an interagency process where we are gathering all of this information. We reach out to the nongovernmental organizations so that they can send in information.

The information gathering part of putting the United States into the report has been, I think, a very good thing as we have been able to hear more about what is happening in the U.S.

In many ways, it is kind of like a doctor who has everybody take their blood pressure when they come to the doctor's office but has for years not had his own blood pressure taken.

We are telling other countries that these minimum standards were the way to go, 11 minimum standards that range from, you know, what kind of laws do you have, what kind of victim protection do you have, et cetera, and not doing that own diagnostic test on ourselves I think was actually hampering us.

So there is a reason far beyond simply the it is fair to look at ourselves if we are going to look at everyone else. But that is also a reason. So the notion of being able to talk to other governments and say look, you know, we have critical language in our own narrative.

When you are looking at your situation you have to be willing to put critical analysis of your own trafficking circumstances out in public and if you are not willing to do that you are going to be hampered. You are going to always have that one anti behind your back.

And so we have seen now in Europe especially the creation of monitoring mechanisms whether it is a totally independent rapporteur like they have in the Netherlands, whether it is a entity like in Belgium with the National Human Rights Foundation, which is a de facto rapporteur, or whether it is somebody who is kind of a trafficking coordinator who has to put out a report.

The Tier I countries especially we are seeing that notion of self-critical reporting being one of the things that differentiates a Tier II country from a Tier I country. So I do think it has had a good effect here in the United States.

Ms. BONAMICI. Terrific. Thank you. Now, I also want to ask you, we have heard a lot about the unaccompanied minors appearing at the border -- frequently discuss that here in the capital and I wonder if you could speak a little bit to the situation in their home countries and the extent to which the situations in those countries might be causing a push factor. Might some of them be fleeing the types of situations we are hearing about today?

AMABSSADOR CdeBACA. Well, one of the things that we have seen in Central America is this notion of the human trafficking problem being a very multifaceted one.

In El Salvador, Guatemala and Honduras you have got countries that have emerged over the last 20 years from civil strife whether it is the dictatorship in Honduras, whether it is the civil war, certainly in the generation-long civil war in Guatemala or in El Salvador and so the level of violence has now been replaced in some ways not as political violence but as gang-related violence and people are afraid.

We have had good conversations whether it is on my own trips to the region or through our embassies with the community groups that are working with families who are facing the notion of the gangs coming by to scoop up their children and not just for prostitution, not just for human trafficking in the ways that many people think of but even for forced criminal activity which is a form of trafficking under the international law.

And so this is, I think, something that we recognize that we need to deal with is, you know, the idea of these factors that are driving and impelling the destabilization, driving the fear that we see in some of these towns.

It very much comes back to the notion of rule of law and I think that what you are seeing from us is not just anti-trafficking projects in Central America but general rule of law projects through the INL, the International Narcotics and Law Enforcement Bureau, being able to come in and start funding policing projects that look to community policing, that look to the ability of police to investigate a case, to ask questions -- not to simply stand back, as is the practice in Latin America, and wait for what is called a denuncia, basically a denunciation, the victim coming in and actually saying, "I am a trafficking victim and that is the person who trafficked me." We found around the world that if you wait for that you are never going to have any trafficking cases. And so working with the Central American governments over the last few years we are starting to turn the needle on that a little bit so that there is more proactive work that protects those vulnerable communities.

And then with the other hand -- with our public assistance funding -- we are actually able to go in with groups like Casa Alianza and others who are serving those at-risk street children that are serving trafficking victims who are coming out of prostitution or other horrible offenses.

And so we are trying to make sure that we can address the root causes on the one hand, address the criminal justice response on the other hand and then we will have a third hand -- help the victims through these NGOs.

Ms. BONAMICI. Terrific. Thank you very much.

Mr. Lowenthal.

Mr. LOWENTHAL. Thank you, Madam Chair, for holding the hearing and I am really pleased to be here and to learn more about not only the whole issue of human trafficking but especially around forced labor and labor trafficking, and I thank you for that very complete kind of overview and report.

I have a couple of questions that I wanted. Now, on the report you mention -- you know, when we talk about Tier I, Tier II and Tier III countries and Tier II, especially those that really do not comply with minimum standards, making some efforts to change, you know, I wonder and especially those countries that have a great deal of gang activity and forcing children and young people to engage in it, do we have any understanding?

Right now we have -- there are three -- there are a lot of Central American young children crossing our borders from both Guatemala, Honduras and El Salvador, all three of those countries being on Tier II.

Do we have any understanding of how many of these children are escaping or are families that wish them to escape from forced labor kinds of things or engaging in activities that the families find extremely dangerous -- that these children are really leaving because of that and are we pursuing that and trying to understand that relationship?

AMABSSADOR CdeBACA. One of the things that has allowed us to, I think, do that much more over the last few years is the Trafficking Act of 2008 and what it sought to do was to enshrine this notion of the best interest determination. We look at the best interest of the child.

Say, for instance, if a Child Protective Services intervention here in the Washington, D.C. or in the suburbs regardless of where the child is from the first thing that you are supposed to ask is what is in the best interest of this child, and that really was the genesis of the Section 4 of the Trafficking Victims Protection Reauthorization in 2008 which was let us make sure that we are looking at this not simply through a security lens but also through the humanitarian lens, through this lens of the best interest determination, and so it provides for time in which to do exactly that.

So the screening that is done whether it is by Customs and Border Protection agents or whether it is done over time by the folks from Health and Human Services this is, I think, an important safeguard so that we make sure that there is that ability to do that screening.

I can't tell you exactly what the results of those are. That is not something that we do. But I think that one of the things we have seen and we have heard certainly the anecdotal reports of parents who are sending their kids north or grandparents who are sending the children north to be with their families because of the gang violence, because of the trafficking and simultaneously we have seen the reporting in -- from our diplomats each year as to what is happening.

Now, the fact that it is a Tier II is looking at what are the government structures and what has the government done as opposed to how bad is the problem of trafficking in that country.

How bad the problem is is not what puts you on the tier. It is what the government is trying to do, and over the last few years we have seen good things from each of those governments that enable them to come off of the Tier II watch list whether it is new laws, whether it was new task forces, whether it was bringing together the different ministries, et cetera.

Tier II is a very large tier. It is kind of the bell curve. It is the bell of the bell curve and there are Tier II countries that are almost Tier III countries and there are Tier II countries that are almost a Tier I country. So I think that in all three of these countries we feel like there is a long way to go to be able to say that trafficking victims are protected in their home towns.

Mr. LOWENTHAL. If someone is seen -- either adjudicated through an immigration court or by -- at a border by Customs or Homeland Security or Health and Human Services to be a victim of human trafficking are those potential grounds for asylum in the United States?

AMABSSADOR CdeBACA. Well, one often wouldn't even get to the asylum analysis if there is a conclusion that the person is a victim of trafficking because then they can go into the Trafficking Victims Service Response, which is in some ways more -- it is not more generous than the asylum response because what we did with the 2000 law was to open up the asylum response to trafficking victims.

But it ends up moving them into a situation where the immigration decisions are not in an adversarial process. The asylum and refugee claims are still an adversarial process. The human trafficking claims are an application to citizenship and immigration services where the people who are experts in both human trafficking and in the cases of battered immigrant spouses.

So it is that unit that handles these. It is very knowledgeable about issues of power, Stockholm syndrome, dependency, vulnerability -- those are the adjudicators at the immigration service that would look at the petitions for the immigrant status for trafficking victims.

And so while some have at times looked at the asylum and said well, we need to have trafficking as a grounds for asylum, when I look at it I look at countries around the world that have tried to route all of the trafficking victims through the asylum process and it inadvertently puts them in an oppositional nature against the government who is having to question whether they are asylees in the first place.

So I think that what we see is if there is a way to look at these situations and say this is actually a trafficking victim then hopefully they go through continued presence, they go through the T visa, they get certified by HHS.

They are also -- HHS has its provisions for unaccompanied alien children, which is the placements and everything else if the person who is truly unaccompanied has no family, even foster care situations.

A number of trafficking victims have been able to take advantage of that -- those placements, et cetera, over the last years. So on the one hand, there is the asylum fears that need to be looked at but there is also if there is a human trafficking fear.

Mr. LOWENTHAL. Thank you. The other -- if I may continue, we are now going to be potentially fast tracking a number of trade agreements and one of them being the TPP, and I know that recommendations have been made regarding the TPP that those that, for example, others that are on the list Tier II -- Vietnam, one, Japan -- that we make sure that we ensure that there are labor standards in the TPP.

But even before that would you recommend that the Congress look at -- ensure that countries make improvements before we even allow them to go forward here? We are going to have -- move forward with trade agreements which potentially could benefit both countries on support of the concept. But I also have real concerns about rewarding bad behavior. Can you comment on that?

AMABSSADOR CdeBACA. I certainly can. My office, of course, is not the office that works on the trade issues and I would certainly defer not only to the USTR but also the folks in what we call our E family that reports to the undersecretary for economics.

But this notion of labor protections and labor rights in part of the negotiations and as part of the agreements is a very important one and I know that there was a meeting just a few weeks ago in Canada as part of the negotiations. I have to admit I was on the road and I haven't been briefed as to how those negotiations went.

It is something we can probably circle back with you on. But I think that, you know, one of the things that we know is that the countries of the Pacific Rim, again, none of them do not have a slavery problem. Whether it is your Tier I countries like Chile or the United States, whether it is Tier II or even your Tier III countries like Malaysia, we are all talking about countries that have to look at this.

And I think that not only having it with the labor protections that are already being negotiated and they are to be built in but then also making sure that the enforcement side ends up coming into play.

One of the things that I continually hear from the Customs guys is that the 1930s Tariff Act and its prohibitions of importation of slave-made goods has not caught up to the Trafficking Victims Protection Act.

And so they sometimes are wondering how can we keep the shipping containers from coming into the United States. It goes back, I think, the chairwoman's point about enforcement. It is not just about having these things on paper.

It is making it so that they can be enforceable, and so I think that that is one of the things that two-tracking -- talking with our TPP and other free trade partners, making sure that these discussions are being had as far as labor standards but then also making sure that on the back end that our guys on the front line, especially at Customs and Border Protection, have a way to deal with these things when they are -- somebody is trying to bring them into the U.S.

Mr. LOWENTHAL. Finally, my third question is -- yes?

Ms. BONAMICI. Excuse me, Representative Lowenthal. Can I ask you to submit that for the record? Because we have another panel --

Mr. LOWENTHAL. Oh, we do? I am sorry.

Ms. BONAMICI. -- and the -- yes, we do have another panel and the ambassadors have provided us with a lot of very thorough information but we would also like to hear from the next panel. So thank you very much, Mr. Ambassador. Really appreciate what you have brought to the discussion and your expertise.

AMABSSADOR CdeBACA. Thank you, Madam Chair.

Ms. BONAMICI. And as we are preparing for the second panel, in the interests of time each of our panelists this morning has a very lengthy bio because of all the work that they have been doing and as we are transitioning I am going to start by giving just a portion of those lengthy bios so you know who is going to be on this next panel.

We are going to hear from Neha Misra. Neha is the senior specialist for migration and human trafficking at the Solidarity Center, which is an international organization that promotes workers' rights. She has spent some time at the United States Department of Justice as did the ambassador.

We are also going to be hearing from Dan Viederman. He is the CEO of Verite -- I am probably going to mispronounce that -- that helps NGOs, governments, investors and multinational companies improve working conditions and eliminate human rights violations.

We are going to hear from Mr. Jesse Eaves, the senior policy advisor for child protection at World Vision, an advocacy organization that assists survivors of human trafficking, and finally, we are going to be hearing from Mr. Biram Dah Abeid.

He is the founder and president of the Initiative for the Resurgence of the Abolitionist Movement in Mauritania. Mr. Dah Abeid's work to combat slavery has helped free hundreds of modern slaves.

And again, we are going to ask that any written testimony will be included in the record, will also be submitting your oral testimony and we appreciate your -- very much your being here and look forward to your testimony.

And I know that there -- different time frames been given to you but I just want to emphasize that if you can keep your remarks concise we will have plenty of time for discussion.

But let us start with Ms. Misra.

STATEMENTS OF NEHA MISRA, SENIOR SPECIALIST, MIGRATION AND HUMAN TRAFFICKING, SOLIDARITY CENTER; DAN VIEDERMAN, CEO, VERITE; JESSE EAVES, SENIOR POLICY ADVISOR FOR CHILD PROTECTION, WORLD VISION; BIRAM DAH ABEID, FOUNDER AND PRESIDENT, INITIATIVE FOR THE RESURGENCE OF THE ABOLITIONIST MOVEMENT IN MAURITANIA

STATEMENT OF MS. MISRA

Ms. MISRA. Thank you so much --

Ms. BONAMICI. Can you please push our microphone button? Thank you.

Ms. MISRA. Good morning. I would like to say thank you, Chairwoman Bonamici and Representative Lowenthal, for inviting the Solidarity Center today to testify at this hearing and in particular I would like to say thank you to Sara and the staff of the Tom Lantos Human Rights Commission for putting this together.

Building upon more than 20 years of experience in the areas of child labor, migrant worker exploitation and supply chain accountability, my organization, the Solidarity Center, raises awareness about the prevalence and underlying causes of forced labor and other forms of trafficking for labor exploitation and implements programs with partners from myriad sectors to combat the problem.

Our anti-trafficking programs span the globe and while each country we work in has its own unique circumstances and problems we have found a common theme. Human trafficking and forced labor have at their core violations of worker rights and lack of labor standards and protections for workers.

Understanding this link between worker rights violations and human trafficking is key to eradicating this horrific human rights abuse globally.

This means that to eradicate forced labor we must address the underlying vulnerability of workers to exploitation, expand and enforce labor laws and allow workers to organize, to monitor their workplaces and improve their wages and working conditions.

In other words, end worker exploitation to end human trafficking. While governments used to be the primary perpetrators of forced labor, the International Labor Organization now estimates that among the 21 million people in forced labor globally the vast majority are exploited in the private economy.

Trafficking for forced labor thrives in a context of private actors and economic coercion. Our response, therefore, must address this context, recognizing human trafficking as more than just sexual exploitation and more than just organized crime.

We must exert economic pressure as a response and recognize the protection of worker rights as key to trafficking prevention. We also must reject policies and practices that restructure and institutionalize harmful economic and business models that increase worker vulnerability to human trafficking.

I would like to give you two examples today to explain what I am talking about. I am going to pick on two countries that were Tier III in the TIP report -- Malaysia and Thailand -- and Representative Lowenthal, you already raised one of the issues that I wanted to bring up regarding the trade agreements, the TPP in particular.

Malaysia this year in the TIP report was downgraded to Tier III and we think justifiably. While the Malaysian economy thrives on cheap migrant labor, foreign workers in sectors such as agriculture, construction, service, manufacturing and domestic work often have their rights violated with little recourse under Malaysian laws, policies and practices.

The Malaysian government has actually implemented policies recently that are increasing migrant workers' vulnerability to forced labor rather than decreasing.

For example, a Malaysian government policy implemented in January 2013 places the burden of paying immigration and employment authorization fees on foreign workers rather than on employers, increasing the risks of debt bondage.

And as you indicated, Representative Lowenthal, the U.S. is currently negotiating the Trans-Pacific Partnership agreement with Malaysia despite these -- their disregard of worker rights and their Tier III ranking.

We think it is absolutely crucial for Congress and the USTR to ensure that bilateral and multilateral trade agreements like the TPP contain labor standards and protections to prevent trafficking, ensuring that standards apply to all workers including migrants.

And as you indicated, Congressman, we think that labor standards in trade agreements should include the same enforcement and dispute resolution mechanisms as other provisions such as intellectual property rights and not be relegated to side agreements, for example.

Given our globalized economy, the link between worker exploitation and human trafficking in the context of forced labor perpetrated by private actors through economic coercion means that products made with forced labor are ending up on our grocery and retail shelves, and governments and businesses are not doing enough to ensure the supply chains are not tainted with forced labor and other forms of human trafficking.

Again, I will give an example of a Tier III country, Thailand. In 2008, the Solidarity Center released a report entitled "The True Cost of Shrimp." Thailand is one of the main exporters of shrimp to the United States.

The report highlighted how companies in Thailand systemically used the lack of labor rights and weak labor law enforcement to exploit the mostly Burmese shrimp processing workers. The report uncovered human rights abuses in the industry such as unpaid wages, unsafe and unhealthy workplaces, child labor, forced labor, physical intimidation, violence and sexual abuse.

Six years after the report, little progress has been made to clean up the industry. Reports continue to surface about human trafficking of migrant workers in the seafood processing sector in Thailand.

Just this year, the Guardian newspaper conducted a six-month investigation and found that a large number of migrant workers were bought and sold like slaves and held against their will on Thai fishing boats.

The Guardian found that such forced labor plays an integral part in the production of shrimp sold in leading supermarkets around the world including in the United States in stores such as Wal-Mart and Costco.

U.S. multinational corporations may be complicit in this. As I said earlier, Thailand is one of the largest exporters of shrimp to the United States and as buyers of Thai processed seafood these companies have not done enough to prove to consumers that their supply chains are not tainted with forced labor.

When our report came out in 2008, Senator Harkin asked the Department of Homeland Security to do an investigation. ICE investigators admitted to us that they knew their investigation would not find forced labor in the industry in Thailand because they must notify the Thai government that they are coming to inspect and the Thai government cleansed all the workplaces that they visited.

As Ambassador CdeBaca pointed out, we have a law called the 1930 Tariff Act, but the law has a huge loophole in it called the consumptive demand exception.

Because of the consumptive demand exception and because of the way that ICE conducts its investigations not being allowed to use evidence from the media, NGOs, trade unions, et cetera, to enforce the Tariff Act, the Tariff Act has not been used to prevent forced -- products made with forced labor coming to the United States.

Thailand is also part of the generalized system of preferences for trade status to the United States. The AFL-CIO filed a trade petition this year to ask the USTR to suspend Thailand from GSP preferences and part of the reasons they gave were the forced labor in the seafood sector.

Even in supply chains of products that are mostly for local use or consumption like bricks in South Asia, the model for addressing forced labor and other forms of human trafficking of workers must be holistic, address worker rights more generally and use economic consequences and incentives.

For example, all indications suggest that Pakistan's brick kiln sector is rife with bonded labor, and bonded labor is Pakistan's largest human trafficking problem. While hundreds of workers are freed from debt bondage each year through the efforts of NGOs, the practice goes largely unabated.

Specifically, programs intended to improve the situation of brick kiln workers have been piecemeal at best and none have tried to promote and link brick production to ethical procurement.

The Solidarity Center has an office in Pakistan which is currently implementing a project from the U.S. Department of State where we are implementing a holistic approach with the concept of decent work brick kilns -- kilns that meet a much higher standard than previously advocated by anyone.

The project would bring on board government entities to support ethical procurement of bricks for construction. The government is a major purchaser of bricks and if so motivated it could help ensure that the program is self-sustaining, leveraging infrastructure development funds to ensure social justice through decent work wages and benefits for brick kiln workers. The Solidarity Center is promoting the concept of economic pressure, economic consequences and economic incentives to combat bonded labor in the brick kiln industry in Pakistan.

Through initiatives such as the upcoming FAR Council regulations to implement Executive Order 13627, Strengthening Protections Against Trafficking in Persons in Federal Contracts, and USAID's Counter-Trafficking in Persons policy, the U.S. government is using federal procurement policy as a way to implement important anti-trafficking initiatives in government supply chains. The Solidarity Center and its partners are using similar economic models to urge governments to do the same and private businesses must follow suit.

Thank you very much. I look forward to your questions.

[The statement of Ms. Misra follows:]

Testimony of Neha Misra
Senior Specialist, Migration and Human Trafficking, Solidarity Center
Before the Tom Lantos Human Rights Commission
U.S. House of Representatives
Thursday, July 24, 2014
End Worker Exploitation to End Human Trafficking

Thank you to the Tom Lantos Human Rights Commission for the opportunity to present the Solidarity Center's perspective and approach to combating international human trafficking. We appreciate the Commission's interest in the issue, particularly its emphasis on trafficking for the purposes forced labor and other forms of labor exploitation.

My name is Neha Misra. I am the Senior Specialist for Migration and Human Trafficking at the Solidarity Center, an international non-governmental organization (NGO) that promotes and protects worker rights globally, with programs in more than 60 countries. The Solidarity Center is an allied organization of the AFL-CIO and a member of the Alliance to End Slavery and Trafficking (ATEST). Building upon more than 20 years of experience in the areas of child labor, migrant worker exploitation and supply chain accountability, the Solidarity Center raises awareness about the prevalence and underlying causes of forced labor and other forms of trafficking for labor exploitation, and implements programs with partners from myriad sectors to combat the problem. These programs include initiatives that address each of the four "Ps" that have become part of the anti-trafficking paradigm: prevention, protection of victims, prosecution (or as we prefer to describe it, "rule of law") and partnerships. The Solidarity Center has the unique ability to work across borders, in both countries of origin and destination for trafficked workers, as we have long-term, on-the-ground relationships with local partners. We have implemented anti-human trafficking programs in countries such as China (Hong Kong), India, Indonesia, Malaysia, Nepal, Pakistan, the Philippines, Sri Lanka, Thailand, Jordan, Kuwait, Qatar, Kenya, Sierra Leone, Moldova, and the Dominican Republic.

The Solidarity Center's anti-trafficking programs span the globe. And while each country we work in has its own unique circumstances and problems, we have found a common theme. Human trafficking and forced labor have, at their core, violations of worker rights and lack of labor standards and protections for workers. Whether its low-wage workers in sectors such as domestic work or construction, migrant workers[1] toiling on palm oil plantations or other marginalized groups, such as poor women workers or child laborers, human trafficking is a worker rights issue because it is linked to various forms of labor exploitation. It is one of the worst forms of worker abuse.

Understanding this link between worker rights violations and human trafficking is key to eradicating this horrific human rights abuse globally. This means that to eradicate forced labor, we must address the underlying vulnerability of workers to exploitation, expand and enforce labor laws, and allow workers to organize to monitor their workplaces and improve their wages and working conditions.
In other words, end worker exploitation to end human trafficking.

---

[1] The term "migrant worker" is the internationally accepted term for a person who migrates for employment, whether temporary, seasonal or permanent. In the United States, in everyday language, "migrant worker" may refer to a seasonal or temporary worker, and "immigrant worker" refers to someone who migrates for work on a more permanent basis, or who has residency rights. I will use the term "migrant worker" in my testimony to refer to all workers who migrate for work, regardless of their status or length of stay in the destination country.

We increasingly hear the term "modern slavery" used by advocates, activists, policymakers and the media to describe the different types of exploitation or compelled service children, women and men end up in through the myriad forms of coercion and deceptive practices traffickers use. Terms such as forced labor, debt bondage and involuntary servitude are used to describe severe exploitation that continue today in our modern world, though under a different guise. Instead of shackles and chains, workers are now enslaved through threats, debt and other forms of economic coercion.

While governments used to be the primary perpetrators of forced labor, the International Labor Organization now estimates that among the 20.9 million people in forced labor globally, the vast majority are exploited in the private economy.[2] The ILO also estimates "the total illegal profits obtained from the use of forced labor globally amount to $150 billion per year. The illegal profits are highest in Asia and Developed Economies. This amount exceeds the GDP of many countries around the world."[3]

Modern slavery thrives in a context of private actors and economic coercion. Our response, therefore, must address this context, recognizing human trafficking as more than just sexual exploitation and more than just organized crime. We must exert economic pressure as a response and recognize the protection of worker rights as key to trafficking prevention. We must also reject policies and practices that restructure and institutionalize harmful economic and business models that increase workers' vulnerability to human trafficking.

Migrant Workers High Vulnerability to Human Trafficking

For example, it is common business practice for employers to subcontract hiring and human resources management responsibilities to labor brokers or employment agencies. These labor recruiters are redefining work, compelling workers—who have no other viable opportunities for employment in their home village or country—to pay exorbitant recruitment fees for the "privilege" of laboring under harsh and often inhumane conditions. Many of these migrant workers end up trafficked into forced labor and debt bondage. Despite this proven connection between recruitment fees and vulnerability to forced labor[4], governments and businesses are institutionalizing these practices through increased temporary migration programs and the under- or non-regulation of labor recruiters.

Unsafe migration processes and the lack of labor law and other legal protections for migrant workers make them particularly vulnerable to forced labor, and governments clearly lack political will to do much about it. The potential profits to be made from the global labor migration business—by government officials, employers, employment agencies and labor recruiters—seem to trump initiatives to combat migrant workers' vulnerability.

Malaysia makes an excellent case study for this profits-over-rights model. It is one of the largest destination countries for migrant workers in Asia. There are approximately 2 million documented and 2 million undocumented migrant workers, including Indonesians, Nepalese, Filipinos, Indians, Bangladeshis, Sri Lankans and, increasingly, Vietnamese, Cambodians, Burmese and Laotians. These migrants comprise nearly 30 percent of the Malaysian workforce. While the Malaysian economy thrives on cheap migrant labor, foreign workers in sectors such as agriculture, construction, service, manufacturing and domestic work often have their rights violated with little recourse under Malaysian laws, policies and practices.

Despite the constant demand for cheap migrant labor, as well as an invariable influx of migrants, Malaysia has few concrete policies and laws to protect migrant workers. And existing policies protecting migrants are not enforced, or are enforced inconsistently, and tend to be short-term, temporary fixes. Malaysia has signed bilateral agreements with several of the countries mentioned above, yet these agreements are often weak and difficult to enforce. Migrant workers in Malaysia consistently face serious violations of internationally recognized labor and human rights, including confiscation of passports, restrictions on movement, deceit and fraud in wages (including nonpayment), forced labor, involuntary servitude, debt bondage and other forms of human trafficking. Physical and mental abuse, including sexual harassment and violence, is a common phenomenon. Migrant workers are also denied the freedom of association in policy and practice, which further prevents them from accessing justice because they cannot initiate grievance procedures or use collective bargaining to gain rights in the workplace.

The Malaysian government has actually implemented policies recently that are increasing migrant workers' vulnerability to forced labor rather than decreasing it. For example, a Malaysian government policy implemented in January 2013 places the burden of paying immigration and employment authorization fees on foreign workers, rather than on employers, increasing the risk of debt bondage. Moreover, the Malaysian government periodically implements crackdowns on undocumented migrants, most recently in January 2014, where they conducted massive operations to detain and deport hundreds of thousands of migrant workers. However, the Malaysian government does not have adequate screening procedures to ensure that trafficking victims are not also detained and deported. In addition, the deportations often involve leaving migrant workers literally just over the

---

[2] *ILO Global Estimate of Forced Labor*, http://www.ilo.org/wcmsp5/groups/public/---ed_norm/---declaration/documents/publication/wcms_182004.pdf

[3] *Profits and Poverty: The Economics of Forced Labour*, International Labor Organization, 2014, (http://www.ilo.org/wcmsp5/groups/public/---ed_norm/---declaration/documents/publication/wcms_243391.pdf)

[4] In its *Profits and Poverty* report, the ILO found "the payment of recruitment fees, even to relatives or friends, leads to a higher probability of ending up in forced labor." Id. at p. 44.

border in Indonesia, without any resources or support. Indonesian NGOs report that these migrant workers are then vulnerable to traffickers who promise them new jobs or assistance getting home.

And yet, despite clearly demonstrating a disregard for worker rights and receiving a Tier 3 ranking in the U.S. Department of State's 2014 *Trafficking in Persons (TIP) Report*, Malaysia is currently part of the Trans-Pacific Partnership (TPP) negotiations with the United States and 10 other countries. Because economic consequences can lead to trafficking protections, Congress, the executive branch and other governments must ensure that bilateral and multilateral trade agreements (like the TPP) contain labor standards and protections to prevent trafficking, ensuring the standards apply to all workers, including migrants. Labor standards in trade agreements should include the same enforcement and dispute resolution mechanisms as other provisions such as intellectual property rights, and not be relegated to secondary status.

Global Supply Chains Tainted with Forced Labor

Given our globalized economy, the link between worker exploitation and human trafficking in the context of forced labor perpetrated by private actors through economic coercion means that products made with forced labor are ending up on our grocery and retail shelves. And, governments and businesses are not doing enough to ensure that supply chains are not tainted with forced labor and other forms of human trafficking.

In general, it is difficult to quantify the extent of forced labor in global supply chains. But as those supply chains reach down to more and more suppliers, the chances that trafficked people are in the labor force increase. For example:

- When buyers and multinational corporations demand cheap or unrealistic pricing structures from suppliers, severe labor abuses, including forced labor, often result in their supply chains.[5]
- Similarly, when employers contract out or hire unregulated subcontracted suppliers, or rely on labor recruiters and employment agencies, they should not be surprised to find that they have trafficking victims in their production lines.
- When employers refuse to enforce or claim that it is too difficult to monitor adherence to core labor standards in their supply chains, the probability that they will find forced labor, debt bondage and other severe forms of labor exploitation increases.

In 2008, the Solidarity Center released a report as part of its *Degradation of Work* series titled, *The True Cost of Shrimp: How Shrimp Industry Workers in Bangladesh and Thailand Pay the Price for Affordable Shrimp*. Thailand is one of the main exporters of shrimp to the United States. The report highlighted how companies in Thailand systematically use the lack of labor rights and weak labor law enforcement to exploit the mostly Burmese shrimp processing workers. The report uncovered major human rights abuses in the industry: unpaid wages, unsafe and unhealthy workplaces, child labor, forced labor, physical intimidation, violence and sexual abuse. Six years later, little progress has been made to clean up the industry.

Reports continue to surface about human trafficking of migrant workers in the seafood processing sector in Thailand.[6] The Thai fishing industry has also received harsh criticism for the trafficking of migrant worker men, not only Burmese, but increasingly Cambodians and Rohingya refugees, onto fishing boats.[7] This was a major factor in the downgrading of Thailand to Tier 3 in the Department of State's *2014 TIP Report*.[8] Just this year, the *Guardian* newspaper conducted a six-month investigation and found that a large number of migrant workers were bought and sold like slaves and held against their will on Thai fishing boats. The *Guardian* found that such forced labor plays

---

[5] The pricing structure as a cause of human trafficking cannot be overemphasized, as this is an underlying factor that employers, business, corporations and consumers can all address. As described in the Solidarity Center's report, *The True Cost of Shrimp*: "As a commodity, the price of shrimp fluctuates according to supply and demand, and price pressure is significant all along the supply chain. Retailers, sensitive to the risk involved with importing fresh food, press import companies for faster distribution, acceptable quality and the lowest prices. Importers, aware that market fluctuations can affect prices, leverage their bulk purchasing power to demand speedy delivery from producers. Trapped between producers and importers are labor-intensive shrimp factories. Often, the factories' response to price pressure is to squeeze wages, neglect workplace health and safety regulations, and cut other corners that leave shrimp workers bearing the social cost of affordable shrimp." *The True Cost of Shrimp*, Solidarity Center, 2008, p. 11.

[6] See for example: "Trafficked into Slavery on Thai Trawlers to Catch Food for Prawns," *The Guardian*, June 10, 2014, http://www.theguardian.com/global-development/2014/jun/10/-sp-migrant-workers-new-life-enslaved-thai-fishing.

[7] See "Special Report: "Thailand Secretly Supplies Myanmar Refugees to Trafficking Rings," *Reuters*, December 4, 2014, http://www.reuters.com/article/2013/12/05/us-thailand-rohingya-special-report-idUSBRE9B400320131205.

[8] http://www.state.gov/j/tip/rls/tiprpt/countries/2014/226832.htm

17

an integral part in the production of shrimp sold in leading supermarkets around the world, including in the United States, in stores such as Walmart, Costco, Carrefour and Tesco.[9]

When the Solidarity Center issued its *True Cost of Shrimp* report, we were immediately attacked by Thai shrimp producers and industry associations, who all claimed that they had good labor practices and clean supply chains. The companies also made promises to be transparent and institute measures to ensure that there was no forced labor in fishing and seafood production in Thailand. Yet every year since, the media, unions and NGOs have provided strong evidence of forced labor in the industry. When the State Department ranked Thailand on Tier 3 last month, the Thai fishing industry again claimed the allegations were outrageous.[10] The industry representatives can make these false claims because they know that they likely will not be held accountable by the Thai government or anyone else.

U.S. multinationals may be complicit in this. As mentioned earlier, Thailand is one of the largest exporters of shrimp to the United States. As buyers of Thai processed seafood, these U.S. companies have not done enough to prove to consumers that their supply chains are not tainted with forced labor.

And despite U.S. laws that prohibit the importation of goods made with forced or child labor, Thai shrimp continues to be found at major U.S. retailers and in consumers' freezers. Similar concerns may be raised about products such as ready-made garments from Malaysia, Haiti, Jordan and other countries where there are reports of forced labor and debt bondage in the industry.

The U.S. government must do more to ensure that multinational corporations are held accountable for their practices abroad. And we must increase government scrutiny of imports to ensure goods made by forced labor are not allowed in the U.S. marketplace. This type of economic consequence will be a catalyst for change. The Coalition of Immokalee Workers' *Fair Food Program* is an excellent example of how economic consequences can help to eliminate forced labor and other forms of labor trafficking in an industry.[11]

The 1930 Tariff Act prohibits the importation of goods into the United States made with forced or child labor. This law, however, is rarely enforced as the "consumptive demand exception" weakens it. As required by the 2005 Trafficking Victims Prevention Reauthorization Act (TVPRA), the U.S. Department of Labor "maintains a list of goods and their source countries which it has reason to believe are produced by child labor or forced labor in violation of international standards."[12] Even though many of the goods on the list are produced for export by the identified countries, the list has not been used to enforce the Tariff Act.

After the publication of the Solidarity Center's *True Cost of Shrimp* report, Senator Harkin asked the Department of Homeland Security (DHS) to investigate. U.S. Immigration and Customs Enforcement (ICE) investigators admitted to the Solidarity Center that they knew that their investigation would not find forced labor in the Thai seafood sector because the investigation process is flawed. Currently, ICE must notify foreign governments of their intent to inspect workplaces that export products to the United States. Such notification results in the "cleansing" of these workplaces to remove any signs of trafficking or forced labor. Moreover, U.S. law does not allow evidence collected by unions, the media or non-governmental sources to be the basis for restricting the importation of products made by trafficked or forced labor. This must be reformed. The DHS must review and rework the role of ICE in overseas inspections.

Thailand is one of the largest exporters of seafood to the United States. The AFL-CIO has filed a petition to suspend Generalized System of Preferences (GSP) status for Thailand with the U.S. Trade Representative (USTR). The AFL-CIO has called for a suspension of GSP as a way to incentivize the Thai government to effectively address forced labor and human trafficking, and other labor rights abuses of migrant and Thai workers. Congress should encourage and support the USTR to suspend the GSP and other trade benefits for any country that does not effectively address forced labor. Economic consequences are key to eradicating forced labor. And countries that are habitual abusers of vulnerable workers should face trade sanctions

Multinational corporations' codes of conduct—which are voluntary and unenforceable—have failed to curtail trafficking in many sectors, including garment/textile, agriculture and seafood processing. There is no easy solution to this problem, but we know that a key deterrent is the ability of unions and labor rights organizations to shine a light on these practices through on-the-ground investigations and worker whistle-blowing. It is crucial for the U.S. government support such monitoring efforts and the efforts of workers to report human rights violations in their own workplaces. Ultimately, workers and trade unions must be empowered to monitor supply chains because history shows that abuses in the workplace only end when workers have the power to ensure that their rights under ILO conventions and national laws are respected. Employers and governments must therefore support and respect the freedom of association for workers.

---

[9] See "Revealed: Asian Slave Labour Producing Prawns for Supermarkets in US, UK," *The Guardian*, June 10, 2014, http://www.theguardian.com/global-development/2014/jun/10/supermarket-prawns-thailand-produced-slave-labour. See also "Thailand's Seafood Industry: A Case of State-Sanctioned Slavery?" *The Guardian*, June 10, 2014, http://www.theguardian.com/global-development/2014/jun/10/thailand-seafood-industry-state-sanctioned-slavery.

[10] "Fishery Invites Supply Chain Inspection," *The Nation*, June 25, 2014, http://www.nationmultimedia.com/business/Fishery-invites-supply-chain-inspection-30237027.html.

[11] http://ciw-online.org/slavery/ and http://ciw-online.org/fair-food-program/

[12] http://www.dol.gov/ilab/reports/child-labor/list-of-goods/

Public awareness campaigns and education for at-risk groups are important tools for prevention; but, in and of themselves, they will not eradicate trafficking for forced labor. Together with increased prosecutions and convictions, one of the most effective prevention tools that governments and businesses have is economic pressure. Governments should impose trade restrictions, import bans or other penalties on products made with forced labor, and multinational corporations should exert their significant power as buyers to hold suppliers accountable to supply chains free of forced labor.

Bonded Labor in Pakistan: Using an Economic Model to Combat the Practice

Even in the supply chain of products that are mostly for local use or consumption, like bricks, the model for addressing forced labor and other forms of human trafficking of workers must be holistic, address worker rights more generally and use economic consequences and incentives.

All indications suggest that Pakistan's brick kiln and agriculture sectors are rife with bonded labor wherein women and children are particularly vulnerable. The Asian Development Bank recently estimated that 1.8 million people (1 percent of Pakistan's population) are bonded laborers, though many NGOs place the estimate much higher. Currently, there is a decent work deficit in these largely informal sectors. Workers are poorly remunerated; payments are almost always below the officially declared minimum wage. Deprived of social security coverage, workers repeatedly find themselves taking additional loans to meet medical expenses and for weddings, funerals and other social occasions. Some workers and their families are even sold from one employer to another and may remain in debt bondage for generations. It is reported that bonded labor is Pakistan's largest human trafficking problem; no existing legislative framework adequately addresses internal trafficking, and enforcement of laws to abolish bonded labor has largely remained weak.

Pakistan's 1992 Bonded Labor System (Abolition) Act theoretically freed all bonded laborers and erased their debts. The Act also established criminal sanctions for those responsible for holding workers in debt bondage. However, successive governments have lacked the political will or capacity to enforce the law. While hundreds of workers are freed from debt bondage each year through the efforts of NGOs and other socially conscious organizations, the practice largely continues unabated and is especially prevalent in brick kilns. Donors, NGOs and others have attempted to intervene on behalf of brick kiln workers, but most efforts have lacked a long-term strategy or a holistic approach to the problem. Specifically, programs intended to improve the situation of brick kiln workers have been piecemeal at best, and none have tried to promote and link brick production to ethical procurement.

The Solidarity Center/Pakistan is in the process of fronting a holistic approach with the concept of "decent work" brick kilns (kilns that meet a much higher standard than previously advocated by anyone). The project would bring on board government entities to support ethical procurement of bricks for construction. The government is a major purchaser of bricks, and, if it so motivated, could help ensure that the program is self-sustaining, leveraging infrastructure development funds to ensure social justice through decent work, wages and benefits for brick kiln workers. The cost of the high-road (clean bricks) might be slightly higher than the market's low-road (un-clean bricks), but the extra cost would markedly enhance the quality of life for kiln workers. The concept links donor and state funding for projects to sourcing bricks from labor-friendly "decent work" clusters of kilns. In addition to improving the socioeconomic condition of workers, this initiative is expected to create a safe haven for the production of bricks because new buildings and their builders will not carry the taint of child and bonded labor.

It is Solidarity Center's contention that paying minimum wages, extending social security coverage to workers, allowing them the right to organize and eliminating child labor and forced labor will have minimal implications on owners' profitability. Any "losses" in profit they suffer will be offset by socioeconomic dividends, such as a more motivated and healthy workforce. Additional policy interventions, such as incentives for owners to comply with labor standards through a "social clause"[13] in public procurement framework, can help sustain the decent work agenda in the brick kiln sector. It is expected that increased demand for bricks as part of a public infrastructure development program will raise the market price of bricks significantly, allowing brick kilns to achieve economies of scale and reap larger profits.

Through initiatives such as the upcoming FAR Council regulations to implement Executive Order (E.O.) 13627, *Strengthening Protections against Trafficking in Persons in Federal Contracts* and USAID's Counter Trafficking in Persons (C-TIP) policy, the U.S. government is using federal procurement policy as a way to implement important anti-trafficking initiatives in government supply chains. The Solidarity Center and its partners are using similar economic models to urge other governments to do the same. Private businesses should follow suit.

Recommendations for Initiatives to Combat Trafficking for Labor Exploitation
End worker exploitation to end human trafficking.
Key initiatives to combat trafficking for labor exploitation should include:
1. *Using trade agreements to prevent forced labor (economic pressure)*:

---

[13] The idea is to make an amendment in federal and provincial public procurement laws, requiring government agencies to procure bricks from certified units, which comply with core labor standards.

a. Congress, the executive branch and other governments must ensure that bilateral and multilateral trade agreements (like the TPP) contain labor standards and protections to prevent trafficking, ensuring the standards apply to all workers, including migrants. Because economic consequences can lead to trafficking protections, labor standards in trade agreements should include the same enforcement and dispute resolution mechanisms as other provisions like intellectual property rights, and not be relegated to secondary status.

b. Congress should encourage and support the United States Trade Representative (USTR) to suspend the Generalized System of Preferences (GSP) and other trade benefits for any country that does not effectively address forced labor. Economic pressure is key to eradicating forced labor. And countries that are habitual abusers of vulnerable workers should face consequences.

2. *Prevention through regulation of labor recruiters*:

a. Congress and other governments should strictly regulate labor recruiters and employment agencies, and eliminate worker recruitment fees and shift costs back to the employer. Workers should not be required to pay fees associated with recruitment, the migration process or placement. Employers must be held liable for the abuses of the labor recruiters they hire. In addition, workers must have a way to ensure that a recruiter is legitimate and licensed.

b. To that end, the U.S. Senate passed *Subtitle F: Prevention of Trafficking in Persons and Abuses Involving Workers Recruited Abroad* and similar provisions in *Subtitle I* as part of S. 744 (Immigration Reform) in 2013 is a significant step toward addressing labor trafficking. In the U.S. House of Representatives, H.R. 3344, introduced last year by Chairman Ed Royce, is modeled after *Subtitle F*, and has bipartisan support with over 70 co-sponsors. The Senate and the House of Representatives should make efforts at the earliest possible time to pass such legislation to end fraud in our nonimmigrant visa programs and prevent trafficking in the labor recruitment system. Not only will such a law help to protect migrant workers in the United States, it will also serve as a powerful model for other countries, which need to pass and enforce similar laws and policies.

c. Governments must specifically adopt measures to de-link government officials from recruitment agencies, including measures to address possible conflicts of interest. High level prosecutions of corrupt government officials and owners of labor recruitment agencies would also send a powerful message.

3. *Safe Migration*: The U.S. Congress and executive branch (J/TIP, DRL, DOL, DOJ), along with other governments, should emphasize safer migration processes for workers. This means ending operations that result in mass deportations of undocumented migrant workers without first implementing effective measures to identify and support trafficking victims. It also means ensuring that deported workers are provided with safe passage home. Finally, governments should amend their laws and policies to make it easier for migrant workers to obtain valid work permits and residency documents at little or no cost, in streamlined processes.

4. *The rule of law (prosecutions and accountability)*

a. Governments should increase the number of prosecutions and convictions for forced labor. This means training police and prosecutors to better investigate and prosecute forced labor cases, and protecting police and other law enforcement officials from retaliation by powerful employers, business owners or high-level government officials for bringing cases forward.

b. Governments also should penalize abusive workplaces by strengthening enforcement and penalties against employers who are found to have trafficked workers or who have bought products or raw materials made by forced labor. This means prosecuting employers and imposing stiff penalties. Employers must be held accountable for the abuses of their subcontractors, including labor recruiters, and for abuses in their supply chains.

5. *The rule of law (creating an enabling environment)*:

a. Congress, the executive branch, other governments and multinational corporations should ensure freedom of association—the right to organize, join trade unions and collectively bargain for all workers—regardless of status or nationality, in both origin and destination countries.

b. Freedom of association must be assured in practice and not just law. This means strict penalties for employers who fire, blacklist, retaliate against or collude with government officials to deport, migrant workers who try to organize; and reform of laws that prohibit migrant workers from joining or holding leadership positions in unions, and from participating in collective bargaining.

c. Governments should reform their labor and other laws to include and protect migrant and domestic workers. All workers—whether national or foreign, documented or undocumented—must have equal and full protection of the law. In addition, governments and employers must recognize and enforce all ILO core labor standards, including the freedom of association and right to organize.

d. Congress and the U.S. Departments of State and Labor should promote the ratification and implementation of *ILO Convention 189 on Decent Work for Domestic Workers*, and the *ILO Protocol of 2014 to the Forced Labor Convention, 1930 and its accompanying Recommendation*.

e. Congress, the executive branch and governments in the region should give equal attention not only to passing better laws, but also to implementing, monitoring and enforcing those laws. To do so, governments must enhance the role of labor inspectors. Labor inspectors must be engaged in and be an integral part of law enforcement initiatives to combat human trafficking. In particular, labor inspectors must be given special training to recognize the signs of human trafficking in a workplace, including debt bondage and other forms of economic coercion that result in human trafficking, and to identify victims. Governments must also ensure that there are sufficient numbers of labor inspectors, and that they have the responsibility to inspect all workplaces—including those with high percentages of migrant workers.

f. Congress and other governments must pass national whistleblower protection laws regarding trafficked workers. Also, companies should ensure that there are such protections in company policy all along the supply chain, and advocate to governments for such protections for workers.

6. *Preventing the importation of goods made with forced labor*:

a. DHS should increase scrutiny of imports to ensure goods made by trafficked or forced labor are not allowed into the U.S. marketplace. This includes reviewing and re-working the role of ICE in overseas inspections. Congress should consider holding a hearing on this issue.

b. Congress should amend the Tariff Act of 1930 to remove the "consumptive demand exception." The demand loophole "renders the ban almost useless, since courts have ruled that U.S. Customs cannot block any product unless the U.S. makes enough of it to meet 100 percent of domestic needs . . . The 1930 provision is unsuited to a globalized 21st-century economy that gives importers a wide choice of suppliers. As the dominant force in this new era, the U.S. has an obligation to set the example."[14] Congress and the executive branch should also amend U.S. law and policy to allow evidence collected by unions or non-governmental sources to be the basis for restricting the importation of products made by forced labor.

c. As an immediate protective measure, DHS and Congress should review the importation of Thai seafood under the 1930 Tariff Act.

---

[14] "U.S. Can Help End Child Labor by Amending 1930 Tariff Act: View", *Bloomberg View*, January 2, 2012, http://www.bloombergview.com/articles/2012-01-03/u-s-can-help-end-child-labor-worldwide-by-amending-1930-tariff-act-view.

7. *Supply chain accountability*:

a. Congress should increase pressure on companies to map their supply chains and make such information public. Companies argue that it is too difficult or expensive to completely map their supply chains. If NGOs and the media can do it, however, companies can too. There needs to be a change in business practices.

b. To that end, Congress should pass supply chain transparency legislation, similar to HR 4842, *the Business Supply Chain Transparency on Trafficking and Slavery Act of 2014*, which was introduced on a bipartisan basis by Representatives Maloney and Smith on June 11,, 2014. Such legislation would require companies to report annually to the Securities and Exchange Commission and on their websites on the measures they have taken to address forced labor, human trafficking and the worst forms of child labor within their business operations, including supply chains and labor management, in a way that is consistent with the obligations of businesses as outlined by the UN Guiding Principles on Human Rights. While such legislation would purely be a transparency measure, we see it as a first step toward ensuring forced labor-free supply chains.

c. As an effective way to monitor supply chains for trafficking and forced labor, Congress, the executive branch, other governments and businesses should promote freedom of association and the right to organize, worker agency and worker representation, over codes of conduct and third party monitoring. The *Bangladesh Accord on Fire and Building Safety* and Coalition of Immokalee Workers' *Fair Food Program* are promising models of how to do this.

8. *U.S. government bilateral and multilateral support*

a. Congress and the executive branch should provide support to origin countries (like Cambodia, Indonesia and Bangladesh) to negotiate multilateral agreements with more powerful destination countries (like Qatar, the United Arab Emirates, and Malaysia) to level the playing field for migrant workers. Because of unequal bargaining power and developing countries' desire for remittances and employment abroad for their citizens, bilateral agreements are often weak and provide few worker rights protections. Multilateral agreements may provide more avenues for labor standards.

b. Congress should authorize and appropriate sufficient long-term resources to the Department of State's Bureau of Democracy, Human Rights and Labor (DRL) and Office to Monitor and Combat Trafficking in Person (J/TIP), as well as the Department of Labor's International Labor Office (ILAB) to support government efforts in high-risk countries around the world in their efforts to combat forced labor and other forms of trafficking for labor exploitation. All three agencies have an important role to play in this effort to provide technical assistance to governments and moral and financial support for civil society (including Solidarity Center long-term local partners) to enhance monitoring and implementation of anti-trafficking capacity building programs.

c. Congress should continue to call for the Department of State to strengthen the labor reporting function in its embassies abroad.

9. *Victim Protection*

a. Promote better protection measures for victims. This includes training government officials to recognize and identify victims of forced labor and other forms of labor trafficking, and not detain or deport them as undocumented migrants.

b. Provide compensation to victims, including payment of withheld or back wages.

Thank you, again, for the opportunity to testify and for your help to combat labor trafficking in the United States and around the world. I welcome your questions.

Ms. BONAMICI. Thank you very much for your testimony.
Mr. Viederman.

STATEMENT OF MR. VIEDERMAN

Mr. VIEDERMAN. Thank you and good morning, Congresswoman Bonamici and Congressman Lowenthal. Thanks so much and thanks to the commission as a whole for hosting -- holding this hearing on an issue that we have worked on for a long time, as have others, and is maybe gradually receiving more attention from the private sector.

That is the focus of our work and is the focus of my remarks. But at any rate, the trend seems to be moving in the right direction. So grateful for the chance to add momentum to that.

Verite's work since the 1990s has been to illuminate human rights and labor rights violations in the global supply chains of multinationals as well as their factories and farms from which they supply.

For the most part we work in confidence with our client companies. They give us access to their operations and we tell them what we find and how to solve it.

Beginning in the late '90s, around 1998, we began to see a strong correlation between the presence of foreign migrant workers in facilities -- farms and factories and places as diverse as Mauritius, Madagascar, Saipan, Jordan, Malaysia and Thailand -- and the presence of really serious human rights and labor rights abuses including health and safety violations, restrictions on movement, sexual abuse and harassment, wage underpayment, excessive work hours and other violations -- violations not only of international conventions of international labor laws but also violations of the company codes of conduct themselves, their voluntary commitments.

Further investigation from funders including Humanity United and other led us to quantify the cause of this correlation. Essentially, high levels of debt incurred by migrants paid as fees to third party intermediaries like labor brokers, having borrowed thousands of dollars to pay these labor brokers at often very high rates of interest, securing these loans with what few assets they have, workers cannot risk losing their jobs. A story from a recent investigation in Taiwan illustrates this problem.

At a Taipei shelter recently for vulnerable migrant workers we met a college-trained Filipina named Edz. She was working at cleaning toilets at a factory, despite having been promised a $600 a month job at a cell phone plant. Essentially, $600 a month is more or less Taiwanese minimum wage.

How Edz got to this plant and ended up in a job quite different from what she had expected and why she couldn't leave is the story of forced labor in the global economy, one that is repeated millions of times in numerous other sectors and other countries.

As we probably all know, in the Philippines travelling abroad for a job is big business and also a desirable career path, considering the lack of jobs at home. Edz told us she had a big family and she wanted to help out her sister and her mother financially so she found someone who promised her a good job in Taiwan. She borrowed close to $3,500 from a money lender to pay this labor broker.

After she conducted paperwork, went on a few bus trips around the Philippines, got some visas, undertook a medical exam, she was flown to Taiwan. When she got there she found out that the job paid $325 a month, not the $600 she had been promised, or about $1.15 an hour -- well below the legal wage in Taiwan.

From that income she had to pay over half, $185 monthly -- so over half of her income -- just to service her debt. On top of that, she was charged $50 a month to share a room in a decrepit and dangerous house. Another $40 went to pay the fees for the Taiwanese labor broker who took her passport and held it.

This left her with just over about $50 to cover food, transport and any other expenses she might have faced in Taiwan, a reasonably expensive country. She did not have any money to send home.

Why didn't Edz leave this job? Why don't workers like her simply leave and find other work? The answer is what is at the heart of what makes these paid laborers modern day slaves.

Their debt acts as an instrument of control, binding workers to this facility and this employer. Leaving the job means they will have violated the terms of their visa and become illegal immigrants and, quite interestingly and paradoxically, it is those who went through the process of getting a legal visa who are often most unwilling to leave their jobs and become illegal immigrants even if that were beneficial to them in the short term.

If they become illegal immigrants, certainly, in particular countries like Taiwan and Malaysia, they will be subject to detention and deportation, and in the vast majority of cases like hers employers will keep passports and identity documents and they will frequently charge workers hundreds of dollars to retrieve them in the form of deposits.

So they literally cannot escape. If workers do leave or if they lose their jobs because they asked for safer working conditions, fewer overtime hours or other advocated -- otherwise advocated for themselves, they will have no way to pay back the loans that they took. So in Edz's case she would have lost $3,500.

In many cases, the people who helped facilitate the migration have connections to organized crime so workers have to keep paying their debt or risk the safety of their families back home. All it takes is a simple phone call from someone in Taiwan to a gang member back home in Philippines that Edz is not being cooperative and her family will be threatened.

This is a common story. We met Rafik, a farmer from Indonesia, who sought work in palm plantations in Malaysia. He was offered originally a job paying the equivalent of $444 a month with the potential for overtime and promised a work visa on arrival.

When he got to the site his passport was taken away, he was presented with unreachable quotas and forced to live in squalid conditions. He and a group of other workers objected to their treatment. The labor contractor had them arrested. He spent 10 months in detention and went home at a total loss of about $2,500 to him.

It is importantly not just businesses and supply chains that face these risks. Migrant workers build infrastructure projects, universities and museums in Abu Dhabi, Olympic and World Cup infrastructure in Russia and Qatar and provide services at U.S. government facilities abroad.

Any sector that employs migrants runs a serious risk of employing slaves. It is also vital that we highlight the connection between human trafficking and corruption risks, an issue that is of great concern and should be of greater concern to companies.

Agents and brokers who facilitate migration pay bribes to an assortment of players in the foreign labor supply chain including complicit employers and also government officials from labor, immigration, border control and law enforcement authorities in both source and destination countries.

These kickbacks and bribes are funded by illegal and excessive fees charged to workers. Indeed, the connection between modern-day slavery and corruption is a risk not only to workers but also for the companies that employ them.

Fortunately, these problems can be solved but they can't be solved by standard corporate social responsibility practices. Forced labor is a hidden problem.

Employers don't want you to know about it and sometimes themselves are not fully aware of how they are connected to the illegal and brutal practices of traffickers who are connected to the provision of labor.

And, of course, workers are afraid to speak up lest they lose their jobs and are forced home deeper in debt than when they arrived. For multinationals and their suppliers, the steps to resolution are clear. I should say the initial steps to resolution are clear.

The first step is that companies have to identify where are migrants working in their supply chains. How did those migrants get there -- what conditions do they face -- what recruitment agents facilitated their migration in the home country and in the country of employment -- how much debt do the workers carry with them -- who do they owe that debt to -- which government officials, if any, were bribed to facilitate migration -- do workers have access to their passports -- is there a credible mechanism by which they can alert someone that they are in need of protection.

So the first step for companies to take is to identify where they face this problem and what the nature of the problem is. Companies need to set clear policies that prevent workers from paying fees to get a job and providing full access to passports so that workers can leave their employer.

Corporate policy must restrict or eliminate the ability of any supplier in its supply chain to force a worker to pay a job -- pay a fee to get a job. Companies need to build understanding and capability among employers on how to meet these policies.

They need to ensure that employers only recruit through labor brokers who can demonstrate the understanding and capability to treat workers fairly and lawfully, including accessing government-run direct hiring programs on a bilateral basis.

And lastly, they should share information throughout industry sectors so that shared exposure to unethical recruiters can be acted on jointly, eliminating the market for unethical and exploitative recruitment. A couple of examples of where this is happening -- through concerted effort by and focus over four years in partnership with our organization Verite, Apple has facilitated the reimbursement by third parties of over $16 million to workers who paid excessive fees to work at Apple suppliers in Asia -- in addition, some of the largest retailers in the world committed to piloting our framework for ethical recruitment among their agriculture suppliers in the U.S. and overseas.

Apparel companies have begun to conduct risk-based due diligence on Taiwanese and Philippines-based brokers. In doing so, these companies are taking important first steps, and sometimes second and third steps, to eliminate the risks faced by workers to support better human resources practices among their business partners and to eliminate a host of illegal and unethical middlemen -- the recruiters -- from their operations.

These businesses do not benefit financially from the presence of these recruiters. They actually carry all the risk without necessarily facing a lower price from their suppliers.

An emerging regulatory regime strengthens the pressure of companies to take action. The California Transparency and Supply Chains Act -- the executive order that Neha just mentioned a second ago -- and the mooted Federal Transparency and Supply Chains Act all seem to be compelling corporate action in a way that we find quite powerful.

From our perspective, this is a problem that is severe and widespread. The solutions are at hand and what we need is more companies to begin to take effort to take the first step to find out where these problems exist in their supply chain.

Thank you for your time and attention.

[The statement of Mr. Viederman follows:]

Testimony by Dan Viederman
CEO at Verité
Hearing: Modern-Day Slavery and What We Buy
United States Congress Tom Lantos Human Rights Commission
July 24, 2014

Mr. Co-Chairmen McGovern and Wolf, and other distinguished members of the Tom Lantos Human Rights Commission, I'm honored to be able to speak before you today to present Verité's perspective on the continued presence of modern-day slavery in corporate supply chains and what needs to be done to eliminate it.

Verité's work since the 1990s has been to illuminate human rights and labor rights violations in the global supply chains of multinationals and their supplier factories and farms. For the most part we work in confidence with client companies – they give us access to their operations, and we tell them what we find and how to solve it.

Beginning in 1998, during the conduct of so-called labor audits, we noted the correlation between the presence of foreign migrant workers on short-term contracts and serious labor rights abuses: health and safety violations, restrictions on movement, sexual abuse and harassment, wage underpayment, excessive working hours and other violations of international conventions, national labor law, and corporate Codes of Conduct.

Further investigation – from visionary funders including Humanity United – led us to quantify the cause of this correlation: high levels of debt incurred by migrants paid as fees to third party intermediaries like labor brokers. Having borrowed thousands of dollars to pay these labor brokers at high rates of interest, securing these loans with what few assets they have, workers cannot risk losing their jobs.

A story from a recent investigations in Taiwan illustrate the problem. At a Taipei shelter for vulnerable migrants, we met a college-trained Filipina named Edz. She was working cleaning toilets at a factory, despite having been promised a $600/month job at a cell phone plant. How she got there, and why she couldn't leave, is a story of forced labor in the global economy, one repeated millions of times in numerous other countries and industry sectors.

In the Philippines traveling abroad for a job is both big business and a desirable career path, considering the lack of jobs at home. Edz has a big family and wanted to help them out. She met a recruiter who promised her a good job in Taiwan. She borrowed close to $3500 from a money lender to pay this labor broker. After a bunch of paperwork, a medical exam and a few bus trips, she flew to Taiwan.

When she reported for work, she found out the job paid about $325 a month, or $1.15 an hour (well below the legal wage in Taiwan). From that income, she had to pay $185 monthly – over half her income — to service her debt. She was charged $50/month to share a room in a decrepit and dangerous house. Another $40 went to pay the fees for the Taiwanese labor broker, who took her passport. This left her with just over $50 to cover food, transport and any other expenses per month. She didn't have enough money to send home.

Why didn't Edz leave? Why don't workers like her simply find other jobs? The answer is the heart of what makes these paid laborers modern-day slaves. Their debt acts as an instrument of control, binding workers to this facility and this employer. Leaving this job means they will have violated the terms of their visa and become illegal immigrants, subject to detention and deportation. In the vast majority of cases like hers, employers keep passports and identity documents – and frequently charge workers hundreds of dollars to retrieve them. If workers do leave — or lose their jobs because they asked for safer conditions or fewer overtime hours, or otherwise advocated for themselves beyond the patience of the employer – they will have no way to pay back the loans that they took. In many cases, the people who helped facilitate their migration have connections to organized crime, so workers have to keep paying their debt or risk the safety of their family back home. All is takes is a simple cell phone call from someone in Taiwan telling a henchman in the Philippines that Edz is not being cooperative and her family back home is harassed.

The story of Edz is a common one in multinational supply chains. Rafiq was a farmer from Indonesia who sought work in palm plantations in Malaysia. He was offered a job paying US$444 a month with the potential for overtime, and promised a work visa on arrival. When he got to the site, his passport was taken away, he was presented with unreachable quotas and forced to live in squalid conditions. When he and a group of workers objected to their treatment, the labor contractor had them arrested for improper work visas. He spent 10 months in a detention camp before finally being sent home, at a total loss to him of over $2500.

It is not just businesses that face these risks. Migrant workers build universities and museums in Abu Dhabi, Olympic and World Cup infrastructure in Russia and Qatar, and provide services at US government facilities abroad. Any sector that employs migrants runs a serious risk of employing slaves. Verité's on-the-ground work in global supply chains routinely uncovers situations where unethical labor brokers and corrupt government officials are instrumental in greasing the wheels to traffic migrants into situations that amount to forced labor. These agents and brokers pay bribes to an assortment of players in the foreign labor supply chain including complicit employers and government officials from labor, immigration, border control, and law enforcement authorities in source and destination countries.

These kick-backs and bribes are funded by the illegal and excessive fees charged to workers. Indeed, the connection between modern-day slavery and corruption is a risk not only for workers, but also for the companies that employ them -- – where corrupt payments to foreign government officials result in an indirect or direct benefit to an employer such as cheap migrant labor, a company could find itself violating the Foreign Corrupt Practices Act.

Behind these stories are statistics. According to the ILO, around 14M people are in conditions of forced labor for economic (as opposed to sexual) exploitation; 9M of them entered forced labor after they migrated either domestically or internationally. As you can see from the examples I have given and those shared by others, the problem of recruitment related debt bondage spans the globe, is seen in multiple sectors and at all levels of the supply chain largely because it is linked to pervasive outsourcing of recruitment, which happens as much in developed economies as it does in the poorest countries. So, the problem of forced labor today indeed affects the most vulnerable people desperate for work, but does not happen only in the poorest countries or the most miserable work sites.

The good news is that these problems can be solved, but not by standard 'corporate social responsibility' practices. Forced labor is a hidden problem – employers don't want you to know about it and sometimes themselves are not fully aware of how they are connected to the illegal and brutal practices of traffickers who are connected to the provision of labor, and workers are afraid to speak up lest they lose their jobs and are forced home deeper in debt than when they arrived. For multinationals and their suppliers, the steps to resolution are clear:

• Identify where migrants are working, how they got there and what conditions they face: what recruitment agents were used in the home country and in the country of employment? How much debt are they carrying and to whom? Were government officials bribed to facilitate their migration? Do workers have access to their passports? Is there a credible mechanism by which they can alert a trustworthy, neutral group that they are being exploited?

• Set clear policies that prevent workers from paying fees to get a job and providing full access to passports so that people can leave their employer.

• Build understanding and capability among employers on how to meet those policies.

• Ensure that employers only recruit through labor brokers who can demonstrate the understanding and capability to treat workers fairly and lawfully.

• Share information throughout an industry sector so shared exposure to unethical recruiters can be acted on jointly, eliminating the market for exploitative recruitment. This can be done. Through concerted effort and focus over four years in partnership with Verité, Apple has facilitated the reimbursement of over $16 million to workers who paid excessive fees to work in Apple suppliers in Asia. Some of the largest retailers in the world have committed to piloting Verité's framework for ethical recruiting among their agriculture suppliers. Apparel companies have begun to conduct risk-based due diligence on their Taiwan and Philippines-based brokers. In doing so, these companies are eliminating the terrible risks faced by workers, supporting better human resources management among their suppliers, and eliminating a host of illegal and unethical middlemen – the recruiters – from their operations.

An emerging regulatory regime strengthens the pressure on companies to take action. The California Transparency in Supply Chains Act required much-needed disclosure; President Obama's Executive Order Strengthening Protections Against Human Trafficking in Persons in Federal Contracts has mobilized investigations by companies that had until now never considered the risk of trafficking in their operations; increasing evidence linking trafficking with risk of corruption and potential violations of the Foreign Corrupt Practices Act has broadened the concern from one of 'responsibility' to one of 'legal obligation.'

The problem is severe and widespread. The solutions are at hand. We need more companies to recognize their exposure to the problem of debt-bondage among migrant workers, and to start down the path to resolving it. We are grateful that the Tom Lantos Human Rights Commission has held this hearing to bring much needed attention to the issue.

Thank you.

Ms. BONAMICI. Thank you for your testimony. Now we will move to Mr. Eaves.

STATEMENT OF MR. EAVES

Mr. EAVES. All right. Thank you, Madam Chairwoman, and thank you, Congressman Lowenthal, for being here. It is a pleasure to be before this commission. As others have said, this commission has been at the forefront of this issue for a very long time and it is a pleasure to be with you today.

World Vision is an international relief, development and advocacy organization that is focused on working with children and their families around the world. We are in about a hundred countries.

We have got about 45,000 employees that are really focused on working with families, their children and their communities to address the root causes of poverty and injustice and that includes forced labor and human trafficking.

We have been asked to testify today about our global experience in preventing and responding to forced labor and human trafficking with a particular focus -- we will focus on two different areas. One is in East Asia and another in a couple countries in sub-Saharan Africa, just to show the diverse nature that forced labor can take.

These two regions in particular are vital and an increasingly influential component of the global economy. Yet, as you know, large areas of both East Asia and sub-Saharan Africa are home to large pockets of the poorest and most vulnerable people on Earth and in both areas the nature of the global marketplace is producing many opportunities to make money in a few nations but is also creating more ways to exploit a person for their labor.

So the opportunity is now and tools are definitely available to make U.S. engagement and funding more coordinated, effective and efficient in tackling this vulnerability.

So together with our partners around the world we can ensure that global economic growth is built on the strengths of a nation's people and not on their backs through bondage. So as in other countries, including America, forced labor takes on many forms and we see children exploited in the textile industry, in agriculture, in construction, in the fishing industry and forced to be domestic servants.

And as my colleagues have already mentioned, it is nearly impossible to address the issue of forced labor and human trafficking without talking about migration. My written testimony contains the full account of Min Min, a Burmese boy who was sold to an Indonesian fishing boat and spent nine years as a slave at sea.

Cases like these have led World Vision to spend a great deal of effort educating communities and especially children that are age 13 through 17. These are children that are most likely to take a job away from home. We educate them on the dangers of risky migration and the proactive status that they can take to prevent themselves from becoming victims.

So, for instance, in Southeast Asia we provide a pocket guide in local languages called the Smart Navigator booklet. So this small easy-to-understand booklet covers what human trafficking is, provides a checklist for ensuring safe travel and even includes basic instructions on how to make an international phone call.

So these simple yet effective steps have come from seeing so many stories like Min Min when migrating to earn money goes wrong.

Our testimony -- our written testimony also focuses on the story of a 13-year-old Ethiopian boy named Wolde. Unlike Min Min, Wolde never left his country and yet was exploited for his labor all the same.

Both Min Min and Wolde were trafficked for their labor to contribute to a supply chain and Min Min contributed to an international supply chain while the cotton shawls that Wolde made were destined for local markets.

However, the goal and the end result were the same -- that free exploitable labor makes inexpensive products for the market place. So labor trafficking taints domestic and international supply chains and threatens companies, consumers and entire economies even. Good and services produced through exploitation pose a high reputational and financial risk to companies and their investors.

Therefore, it is critical for companies to know what goes into the products they make and even more critical for consumers to know what goes into the products that they buy.

So it is highly unlikely that a consumer knew that the fish they were eating or the shawl they were wearing were a product of the forced labor of Min Min and Wolde. And yet it is consumers who hold the big piece of the solution to ending forced labor in supply chains.

So business transparency, as already mentioned, protects workers, companies and consumers. It creates a level playing field so that consumers who want to purchase products untainted by forced labor or exploited labor can reward companies that are making efforts to root out exploitation in their supply chain.

So, obviously, Congress can play a role in creating more transparency by passing H.R. 4842. That is the Business Supply Chain Transparency on Trafficking and Slavery Act of 2014. That is a mouthful.

But it is critical to point out that governments cannot make this progress alone and business transparency legislation will not be a silver bullet and there is no single intervention or effort that can defeat the use of forced labor in human trafficking in the long term. And Congresswoman, you pointed to this in your opening remarks that it takes a multifaceted multi sector approach to combat exploitation and World Vision firmly believes that.

For example, in a project in Ethiopia funded by the U.S. Department of Labor we reach over 20,000 children working in the textile industry and also in agriculture, domestic servitude and other sectors.

The program focuses on protection of these children, education, increasing household income, increasing access to credit and the empowerment of local communities. We also focus on another key factor that most people take for granted and that is birth registration.

Human traffickers pursue individuals who are vulnerable and powerless and without a birth certificate children in particular are invisible to their governments and thus very easy to target and very easy to hide.

The U.S. House has introduced the Girls Count Act, H.R. 3398, to empower the U.S. government to address the importance of birth registration and we definitely thank the co-sponsors of that bill including you, Congressman, for supporting that and taking on this important issue that while it may not seem like it is related is the first line of protection for many of these children and as they get older for adult workers.

The U.S. government currently has multiple options for partnering with governments that wish to really take on the issue of forced labor and human trafficking. So in addition to the diplomatic tool of the Trafficking in Persons report, the U.S. government has tools to build on the recommendations of the TIP report with strategic multi sector bilateral partnerships with focus countries.

I will refer you to my written testimony for a full list of these tools which includes USAID's counter trafficking in persons policy, the action plan for children in adversity and the key provisions of the Child Protection Compact Act, which were included in the Trafficking Victims Protection Act of 2013.

So these tools allow for constructive and coordinated bilateral partnerships that will enable countries to develop and expand their systems of prevention, protection and prosecution and ideally address many of the root causes of trafficking.

So Congress has given the administration good tools and it is critical that we work together so that these tools are not left to rust in the tool box.

So thank you again for holding this hearing and for all the work you all continue to do in addressing forced labor and human trafficking, and we look forward to answering your questions.

[The statement of Mr. Eaves follows:]

Testimony of
Jesse Eaves
Senior Policy Advisor for Child Protection
World Vision USA

US House of Representatives
Tom Lantos Human Rights Commission Hearing
On
Combatting Forced Labor and Modern Day Slavery
July 24, 2014

Thank you, Mr. Chairman, for convening this important hearing and inviting World Vision to testify. This Commission has been a leader in the fight against forced labor, human trafficking, and modern day slavery. We are especially grateful that you have championed programs to protect vulnerable children. Children around the world are alive, and contributing to their communities and countries, because of these programs. Your efforts have led to an increased U.S. focus on displaced children, orphans, children affected by armed conflict, and children trafficked for sex or labor. Thanks to your tireless efforts, America remains a global leader in combatting these and other critical issues that impact and endanger children. This hearing is an opportunity to shine a light on what is happening globally to address forced labor and discuss how the U.S. can strengthen its role as a global partner in those efforts.

World Vision is a Christian relief, development, and advocacy organization serving millions of children and families in nearly 100 countries. Our 45,000 employees are dedicated to working with children, families, and their communities to tackle the root causes of poverty and injustice. This work includes emergency relief and preparedness for people impacted by natural disasters and armed conflict; long-term economic development; preventing and responding to abuse, neglect, exploitation, and violence against children; mobilizing children, youth and local communities to hold their governments accountable; and advocating for effective systems, laws, and policies that protect vulnerable populations where the social fabric is especially weak.

World Vision U.S. has more than one million private donors in every state and Congressional district, partners with over 16,000 churches in the United States, and works with corporations and foundations. We are part of the global federation of World Vision International, which last year implemented more than $2.6 billion in programming to help children and communities through international relief, development, and advocacy assistance. Although private donors support much of our work, the U.S. Government is an invaluable partner. We leverage this partnership to reach many more children at-risk and ensure that the precious resources of the American taxpayer are prudently used to promote and protect the well-being of children and communities abroad.

World Vision has been asked to testify about our experience preventing and responding to forced labor and human trafficking. To highlight the pervasive and diverse nature of labor trafficking, our testimony will focus on what we are seeing on-the-ground, contrasting East Asia and Sub-Saharan Africa: A region that is increasingly vital to the global marketplace and another that has some of the fastest growing economies in the world and hopes to likewise be vital. Yet both regions are deeply and negatively impacted by forced labor and the U.S. has a strong part to play in addressing the causes and the impacts. Our testimony will discuss the U.S. role in combatting forced labor and human trafficking and the impact of programs (U.S. funded and non-U.S. funded) and funding that aim to prevent these crimes. The opportunity is now, and tools are available, to make U.S. engagement and funding more coordinated, effective, and efficient. Together with partners around the world, we can ensure that global economic growth is built on the strengths of a nation's people, not on their backs through bondage.

East Asian countries are essential, increasingly influential components of the global economy. African countries like Ethiopia (in east Africa) and Lesotho (in southern Africa), hope to increase their economic clout. Yet both regions are home to large pockets of the poorest, most vulnerable people on Earth.

According to the International Labor Organization, forced labor and human trafficking is a $150 billion industry. Most media and governmental attention to human trafficking understandably focuses on sex trafficking. However, labor trafficking ensnares more people and makes more money. All of these countries have laws that address human trafficking and fight labor exploitation to varying degrees. However, as in other countries – including America – there is a disconnect between national laws on forced labor and human trafficking and local level implementation and awareness of these laws. In fact, even in countries where there is legislation on labor trafficking, most implementation focuses on sex trafficking (East Asia) or trans-national trafficking (Ethiopia and Lesotho) and often neglects labor trafficking as a priority at the national and local level. As a result, the level of impunity is often high and chances of justice for survivors is often low. There is frequently little reason for employers and traffickers to obey the law. Furthermore, there are multiple root causes for forced labor and trafficking – including household income levels, lack of education, issues of land tenure, and an increasing demand for cheap, unskilled labor – not just one, which makes addressing these scourges more challenging. Every story is different. They all still point to how governments, civil society, and communities can do better to end modern day slavery.

As in other countries, including America, forced labor and human trafficking take many forms. We see children exploited as child soldiers, textile weavers, working in brick kilns, agriculture, construction, the fishing industry, and forced to be domestic servants.

Migration, within and outside a country's border, is a common factor for many of the children with whom we work. In East Asia, the global marketplace is producing many opportunities to make money in a few nations but is also creating more ways to exploit a person for their labor. Moreover, economic growth in countries like Thailand, Indonesia, and Malaysia has not been matched in countries like Myanmar, Laos, and Vietnam. In the high-growth countries, this creates strong demand for low-skilled labor that their own local populations have been unwilling to meet. As a result, a steady supply of cheap, often exploitable, labor moves from one country to another or from rural areas to urban centers. It is nearly impossible to address the issue of forced labor and human trafficking without talking about migration. We have seen families in communities we work with in Cambodia, the Philippines, and Ethiopia, torn apart by high amounts of debt that they take on to pay the fees that unscrupulous employment agencies often require to secure a job abroad. These jobs are often not what was promised and can lead into the dark hole of debt bondage. Understanding and addressing what factors push and pull people toward migrating unsafely are critical to preventing and responding to their vulnerability.

Two stories illustrate the varying, yet similarly deep impacts of migration on human trafficking. As the eldest son from a poor family in Myanmar, Min Min felt the pressure to help his family earn money and survive. He befriended a man who came to his village and told him he could get work in Thailand. When Min Min arrived in

Thailand by boat, he was immediately sold to an Indonesian fishing vessel. He describes his ordeal Hellish. He was forced to work all night and most of the day for seven days a week. He says he watched his captors torture or kill anyone who tried to escape. For nine years, Min Min toiled on the boat until finally, one night, desperate to escape, he slipped off the boat and swam to shore. He found himself in Indonesia with no food, shoes, nor clothes. He made it to a small village. But because he had no visa or identity documents, there was little that the villagers could do for him. Min Min was finally able to call his family and they contacted World Vision. We worked with Myanmar's government to get Min Min back home and end his ordeal. World Vision's End Trafficking in Persons Program (ETIP) provides direct assistance to trafficking survivors like Min to fully recover from the trafficking harm and re-integrate into life in society.

Wolde is from a rural village in Ethiopia. By age 13, he was out of school and often going to bed hungry, because the wages his single mother made from selling crops from her garden were meager. Wolde's uncle convinced him that he could earn money, have new clothes, and give his mother a better life if Wolde would move with his uncle to Sodo, a city in Ethiopia. As soon as Wolde arrived in Sodo, he was taken to a small house where he joined five other children who were even younger than him. Each child was responsible for producing seven *gabis* (traditional cotton shawls) per week. The children toiled from dawn till midnight and their owner beat them if they failed to meet their quota. Wolde recalls one boy who became very sick and could not weave and was taken to another town where he was left on the streets. Wolde eventually escaped and is now part of a World Vision program aimed at assisting children like him.

Both stories illustrate where so much can go wrong and what can be done to help prepare migrants for what they might face when they leave home to work. In Myanmar, Vietnam, and Laos, we have worked with scores of children who were promised a job in another city or another country and found a situation that was nothing like they were promised and were forced into a situation where their inherent human worth and dignity is ignored. Cases like these have led World Vision to spend a great deal of effort educating communities and especially children aged 13-17 (those most likely to take a job) on the dangers of risky migration and the proactive steps they can take to prevent themselves from becoming victims.

For instance, throughout East Asia, we provide a pocket guide in local languages called the "Smart Navigator Booklet." This small, easy-to-understand booklet covers what human trafficking is; provides checklists for maximizing safety while travelling; and even includes basic instructions on how to make an international phone call. In places like Ethiopia and Lesotho, World Vision runs Youth Clubs and local Child Protection Committees that engage and educate young people and their families on the dangers of migrating for work. These simple, effective steps come from encountering so many Min Min's and Wolde's whose migration to earn money goes wrong.

Both Min Min and Wolde were trafficked for their labor to contribute to a supply chain: An international one for Min, while the shawls that Wolde made were destined for local markets. However, the goal and end result were the same – free, exploitable labor makes inexpensive products for the marketplace. It is highly unlikely consumers knew that children were forced to process the fish they were eating or make shawl they were wearing. Consumers are essential for ending forced labor in supply chains. The U.S. Government is also key.

Labor trafficking taints domestic and international supply chains and threatens companies, consumers, and entire economies. Goods and services produced through exploitation pose a high reputational and financial risk to companies and their investors. Therefore, it is critical for consumers to know what goes into the products they buy.

BUSINESS TRANSPARENCY PROTECTS WORKERS, COMPANIES, AND CONSUMERS. IT CREATES A LEVEL PLAYING FIELD, SO THAT CONSUMERS WHO WANT TO PURCHASE PRODUCTS UNTAINTED BY FORCED OR EXPLOITED LABOR CAN REWARD COMPANIES THAT ARE MAKING EFFORTS TO ROOT OUT EXPLOITATION IN THEIR SUPPLY CHAINS. WHILE THE MAIN BURDEN FALLS ON COMPANIES AND CONSUMERS, THERE IS MUCH GOVERNMENTS CAN DO. H.R.4842 – BUSINESS SUPPLY CHAIN TRANSPARENCY ON TRAFFICKING AND SLAVERY ACT OF 2014 – IS AN OPPORTUNITY FOR THE U.S. GOVERNMENT. THIS BILL WOULD REQUIRE COMPANIES WITH GROSS SALES OVER $100 MILLION TO POST ON THEIR WEBSITES, AND SUBMIT TO THE SECURITIES AND EXCHANGE COMMISSION, WHAT THE COMPANY'S POLICIES ARE ON SLAVERY AND EXPLOITATION IN THEIR SUPPLY CHAIN. THE BILL WOULD NOT REQUIRE COMPANIES TO TAKE ANY FURTHER ACTION AND WILL PROVIDE CONSUMERS WITH MORE KNOWLEDGE ON WHAT COMPANIES ARE DOING TO ENSURE THAT SLAVERY DOES NOT TAINT THEIR PRODUCTS. WHILE NOT ADDRESSING EVERYTHING, THIS BILL INCENTIVIZES COMPANIES TO LOOK HARD AT THEIR SUPPLY CHAINS AND MAKE THE EFFORTS NECESSARY TO PROTECT THEIR WORKERS, THEIR BRAND, AND THEIR CUSTOMERS.

As the business transparency legislation shows, there is no single intervention or effort that can defeat the use of forced labor and human trafficking in the long term. World Vision programs are most successful when we take a multi-faceted, multi-sector approach to combatting exploitation.

Often times, the most effective efforts seemingly have nothing to do with forced labor and are aimed at strengthening the systems of complete protection for parents and children. For example, World Vision implements the Ethiopians Fighting against Child Exploitation (EFACE). Funded by the U.S. Department of Labor and running in twelve districts in Ethiopia, EFACE reaches 20,000 children primarily working in traditional weaving and some in agriculture, domestic servitude, and construction. Child labor in Ethiopia results from factors like poverty, lack of access to quality education, cultural acceptance of child labor, debt, migration, and lack of regulation in the informal sector, particularly in traditional weaving. The program aims to remove kids from dangerous or exploitative working conditions and get them back to school through tutoring and catch-up classes.

The focus on education is particularly important. World Vision research found that the higher the literacy level of a child, the more aware they are of human trafficking. World Vision and our local partners then work with children's parents to increase and diversify household income and to provide safe options for saving and obtaining credit. Access to income and credit reduces the incentive to remove a child from school and send him or her to work. Sustainable ways to earn a living create stability for families, making them less likely to migrate to find work or place their children into risky situations. A regional World Vision project in Kenya, Rwanda, Tanzania, and Uganda – a model for the EFACE project and also funded by U.S. Department of Labor – used a similar approach that removed nearly 33,000 children out of the worst forms of child labor or prevented them from even being subjected to them.

World Vision also focuses on another key factor that most people take for granted: birth registration. Human traffickers pursue individuals who are vulnerable and powerless. Without a birth certificate, children are an especially easy target.

According to UNICEF, every year 51 million children are never registered at birth, leaving them without an official name or nationality. There are an estimated 135 million unregistered children in East Asia alone. In Sub-Saharan Africa, the situation is more dire, with only 38% of African children currently registered. Children without a birth certificate are often invisible to their government and thus denied basic opportunities and their lives read like a checklist to human traffickers: poor, no education, unable to access safe credit, separated from family with no identification, and unable to verify their age. Lack of age verification also makes forced marriage easier – an issue in countries all over the world and especially in East Asia and Africa.

Birth registration impacts all aspects of a child's well-being. A birth certificate helps protect children from human trafficking, child labor, early marriage, underage recruitment, and conscription into military service. If a child is abused, neglected, exploited, or exposed to violence, a birth certificate ensures his or her access to services and justice systems. It is also critical for obtaining identity documents needed for trans-border migration for work. It is therefore unsurprising to see that in a World Vision survey, 80% of children in Vietnam, which has almost universal birth registration at 99%, are more aware of the need to travel with identity documents. By comparison, only 60% of children in Burma, which has an 81% registration rate, have such awareness. WV is partnering with Plan International and the UN to organize the Ministerial Conference on Civil Registration and Vital Statistics (CRVS) in the Asia and Pacific in November 2014. This is an opportunity to raise awareness and generate governmental action on the foundation for protecting the well-being of children.

In many African nations, the numbers and the level of vulnerability are much worse. In Ethiopia, an astonishing 93% of the population are unregistered, making them extremely vulnerable to unscrupulous labor recruiters who offer foreign jobs seemingly without the need for documentation like a visa or passport. As noted in the 2014 Trafficking in Persons (TIP) Report, Ethiopia recently put a temporary moratorium on foreign labor recruitment to halt the number of Ethiopians who were taking jobs abroad and falling into exploitation. In Lesotho, only 45% of all children under five years old are registered. World Vision works with the Lesotho government to increase these numbers, especially in rural areas where the low registration rate, coupled with the high number of double orphans (when both parents have died), means that authorities are often unaware that a couple who died of AIDS had any children. This has led to an increase in children living on the street, trafficked for sexual exploitation, or forced to work as domestic servants or cattle herders.[15]

The U.S. Government has multiple options for partnering with governments and civil societies in regions as varied as East Asia and Sub-Saharan Africa to strengthen the overall response to these crimes and prevent them from happening in the first place. In addition to the diplomatic tool of the TIP Report, the U.S. Government has tools to build on the recommendations of the TIP Report with strategic, bi-lateral partnerships in focus countries. For instance, the Trafficking Victims Protection Act of 2013 included the key provisions of the Child Protection

---

[15] "Compacting the Fragments: Strengthening the US Government Approach to Child Protection in the Next Decade." Washington D.C. World Vision US, http://www.worldvision.org/resources.nsf/main/trafficking-report/$file/compacting-the-fragments.pdf

Compact Act (CPCA). This allows the State Department to partner with a government and set measurable goals over a multi-year period to strengthen the protection system for vulnerable children and improve justice systems so they investigate and prosecute those who would exploit a child. This is an exciting opportunity for the U.S. Government to engage deeply on these issues.

Another opportunity lies with the U.S. Agency for International Development (USAID). In 2012, USAID unveiled the agency's Counter Trafficking in Persons (CTIP) Policy. In 2013, they released a field guide for USAID missions to assist in the implementation of the Policy. One of the programming objectives calls for USAID to begin integrating CTIP efforts into larger programming sectors, such as agriculture, health, economic growth, education, and humanitarian assistance. This will enable an increase in anti-trafficking efforts that take the multi-faceted approach that is proving effective at targeting the root causes of vulnerability. Furthermore, another programming objective of the CTIP policy is specific CTIP investments in what USAID calls "Critical TIP Challenge Countries." These are countries that have global, significant strategic importance and have significant trafficking problems. Of particular focus are countries that have spent several years on the Tier 2 Watchlist or Tier 3 of the TIP Report. This creates opportunities for impactful engagement, especially because 14 African countries currently reside on the Watch-list, while nine reside on Tier 3.

Finally, further opportunities exist in the Action Plan for Children in Adversity (APCA). Launched in 2012, the Action Plan unites and aligns 30 offices in seven U.S. Government agencies around the same measurable, achievable goals for international programs relating to vulnerable children. The three main objectives are **strong beginnings** (ensuring children meet early childhood development milestones), **family care first** (making sure every child is in a safe family environment), and **stronger prevention and response** to violence, abuse, neglect, and exploitation. The Action Plan, which USAID currently coordinates, enables U.S. Government agencies to coordinate their efforts to make U.S. programs more effective and efficient. The selection of the first focus countries will provide an opportunity to show how coordinated and multi-faceted programs can collectively contribute to reducing the vulnerability of children.

These tools allow for constructive and coordinated bi-lateral engagement that will enable countries to develop and expand the systems of prevention, protection, and prosecution, and ideally address many of the root causes of trafficking in the region. With the right engagement and approaches, we can mitigate trafficking and eliminate it as much as is possible.

Congress has given the Administration good tools. It is critical that we work together so these tools are used and not left to rust in the toolbox. Thank you again for holding this hearing and for all the work you continue to do in the fight against forced labor and human trafficking. World Vision is committed to working with the Commission on these critical issues and I look forward to answering your questions.

Recommendations

- Encourage the Administration to use bi-lateral tools like the Action Plan for Children in Adversity and Child Protection Compact Act that foster collaboration, sustainably strengthen systems of protection, and produce measurable results.

- Support current U.S. Government birth registration efforts by passing the Girls Count Act (H.R. 3398) and urge the U.S. Government to support the implementation of East Asia Ministerial Plan of Action (2015–2024) that will be finalized during the Ministerial Conference in November 2014.

- Support creating a level playing field for businesses selling goods in the U.S. by passing H.R.4842, the Business Supply Chain Transparency on Trafficking and Slavery Act of 2014.

- Encourage USAID to further roll out their Counter-Trafficking in Persons (CTIP) policy which calls for integrating anti-trafficking efforts into other programs like economic development, emergency response, health, and education, and other steps, and allocates sufficient resources in TIP Challenge Countries.

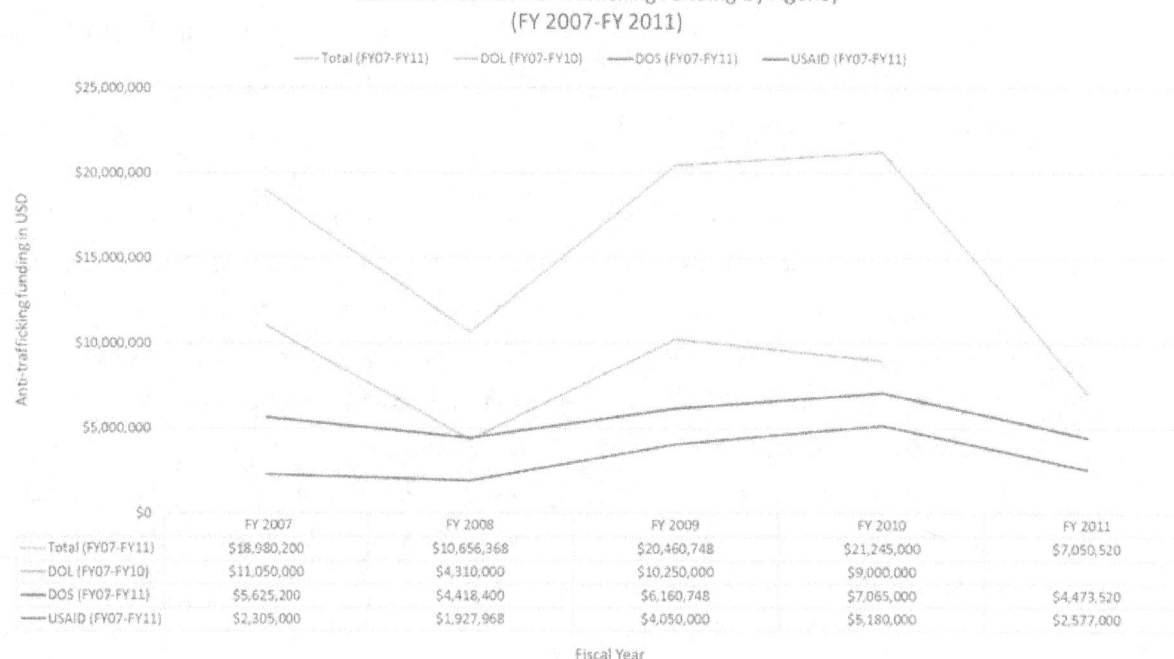

	FY 2007	FY 2008	FY 2009	FY 2010	FY 2011
Total (FY07-FY11)	$18,980,200	$10,656,368	$20,460,748	$21,245,000	$7,050,520
DOL (FY07-FY10)	$11,050,000	$4,310,000	$10,250,000	$9,000,000	
DOS (FY07-FY11)	$5,625,200	$4,418,400	$6,160,748	$7,065,000	$4,473,520
USAID (FY07-FY11)	$2,305,000	$1,927,968	$4,050,000	$5,180,000	$2,577,000

Ms. BONAMICI. Thank you very much for your testimony.

And finally, we turn to Mr. Biram Dah Abeid and please correct me if I mispronounced your name. Welcome. Glad you are here.

STATEMENT OF MR. DAH ABEID

INTERPRETER. He thanks you for being here and he says to avoid a very long testimony in English and French he recommends that I read it for him.

Ms. BONAMICI. That is fine. That is right. That is fine. Thank you.

[The following testimony was delivered through an interpreter.]

Mr. DAH ABEID. Ladies and gentlemen, members of the commission, I am honored to have been invited by your prestigious commission to speak on the theme of modern-day slavery and what we buy, a subject which is particularly dear to me.

This session coincides with a crucial moment in the future of my country in a context of economic crisis and active denial of the practice of slavery and discrimination. Please, thus, allow me to thank you from the bottom of my heart for this wonderful opportunity which you have offered me in order to inform you of daily suffering of slaves and marginalized people in Mauritania.

The Mauritanian population composed of Bambaras, Wolofs, Pulars, Soninkes, Arabo-Berbers and Haratines current live in a society characterized by profound disparity and ancient practices sustained by a system of discriminatory governance and exclusion.

The Haratines, the main victims of slavery, constitute nearly 50 percent of the Mauritanian population. Broadly, this population is poor, uneducated and lives in peripheral communities in Mauritania's main cities and in rural zones.

Both the descendants of slaves and slaves are abused without mercy and are excluded from the institutionalized economic system. Approximately 50 percent of Haratines live in conditions of slavery and are submitted to domestic servitude, forced labor or bonded labor.

They remain marginalized and unrepresented in political posts and in public service. The Haratine make up 80 percent of the illiterate population with 80 percent of Haratines not having completed elementary school and representing only 5 percent of students at institutions of higher education.

More than 90 percent of the dock workers, domestic workers and workers of low-skilled and low-paying jobs are Haratine whereas only 2 percent of high-level officials and senior public and private sector leaders derive from this group.

Full power as well as economic benefits are controlled by the Arabo-Berber community. Foremost, I would like to point out the duplicity which the Mauritanian state and the dominant groups use to scoff at international opinion and make light of the country's partners.

Indeed, modern anti-slavery and anti-discrimination laws are decreed. A roadmap deliberately omitting the existence of the scourge of slavery has been compiled. The country adheres to the principal international instruments for defending human dignity but at the same time the state continues to protect and extend all the privileges solely to the Arabo-Berber community.

The state divides Muslims into masters and slaves and stipulates that the slave is his master's property and that his master can sell him, give him away, use his as security, give him as a gift.

The master thus enjoys the labor of the slave without paying him wages and he has access to the bodies of female slaves against their will, no matter how old they are or how many they are. A master can thus use and abuse his female slaves as he pleases.

This description, not complete, of what is called the Black Code in Mauritania is still in effect and is taught in numerous law schools and divinity schools. It finds itself codified in the books which my organization symbolically burned on April 27, 2012 in Nouakchott, the capital of Mauritania.

IRA-Mauritanie, IRA-Mauritania, and SOS-Slaves, one of the principal and officially recognized anti-slavery organizations in Mauritania, continually work to draw the attention of the authorities on the gross abuses endured by the slaves. But the responses thus far have been far from what we expect.

In 2013, Mauritania put in place a governmental solidarity agency called TADAMOUN. This agency is meant to support victims of slavery but it has been voided of all substance.

Today, the agency is a political propaganda tool completely guided and controlled by those close to masters and stakeholders in the system of slavery. The actions undertaken by this agency are not for the benefit of the real victims.

In reality, all the victims of slavery identified in the regions of Hodhs, Trarza, Assaba, Brakna, Adrar and Nouakchott have never benefited from any assistance from this agency. In these regions, women who have escaped slavery and moved to large urban areas do not receive governmental assistance.

These women are very poor, uneducated, often divorced or never married but have children born from repeated rape by their former masters.

The programs initiated by this agency are very often put in the hands of Arabo-Berber businessmen who are close to power and continue to enrich themselves much to the discontentment of the Haratine masses, poor and bound in servitude, who are the very people these programs are supposed to help.

The true defenders of the rights of slaves are not asked to be part of the conception, management or implementation of the policies of the anti-slavery commission.

In 2013, my country announced the creation of a special court to deal exclusively with slavery and slavery-related crimes. But until today, not one measure has been taken to clarify its composition, where it stands in the legal framework, its prerogatives and guarantees of its independence.

Since the enactment of the law criminalizing slavery in 2007, none of the cases brought before the judiciary have been dealt with appropriately. Take the case of two brothers, Said and Yargue, in 2011 for which only one sentence was handed down.

Today, the case is with the criminal division of the Nouakchott court of appeals due to the liberation of the only convicted person after only three months of detention and then a subsequent annulment of his sentence.

In Mauritania, household servants constitute an extremely exploited marginal population that enjoys no legal protection. In 2011, the country enacted a decree regulating domestic labor but it was not applied and it went unheeded. Cases of human trafficking toward the Gulf countries have been pointed out several times to the state of Mauritania without the state ever taking appropriate protective measures.

Victims of trafficking are generally exploited as household servants or as sex workers. The Mauritanian state has established a patronage system skewed in favor of Arabo-Berbers in all sectors of the national economy -- mining, fishing, manufacturing and more.

The system allocates exclusively to Arabo-Berbers the benefits required for activity in these economic sectors. They thus are able to amass heaping profits which allows domination and exploitation of slaves to continue. Descendants of slaves and Afro-Mauritanians are exploited in these economic sectors and paid meager salaries.

I would like to add that in addition to the practice of hereditary slavery the Mauritanian state also fosters a system that excludes and discriminates against the Afro-Mauritanian community. People responsible in Mauritania for the crime of slavery are protected by the Mauritanian state and enjoy immunity.

More than 30 cases of slavery, and mostly affecting women and children, are pending before national courts without any convictions handed down. Taking advantage of the fear and ignorance of slaves, Mauritanian of courts always use the ruse of paying very small sums of money to victims, disguising this as reparations for being enslaved.

Victims of slavery and injustice in my country need you to convince Mauritania's government to end this political, economic and diplomatic policies of impoverishing and denying justice to vulnerable populations by recognizing the existence of massive scale slavery to which the Haratines are subjected.

In conclusion, they need you to convince Mauritania to cease its hypocrisy and apply its national laws as well as the international laws that Mauritania has fully adopted. We need you to help us abolish the teaching of the valorization of slavery and other forms of inequality that are part of our books and age-old codes and that only our country still grants immunity to today.

To conclude, I would like to pay tribute to all the militants, women and men, of IRA, SOS-Slaves and to all my friends and my family for their sacrifices and loyalty to the cause we defend.

Thank you.

[The statement of Mr. Dah Abeid follows:]

Mr. President,
Ladies and gentlemen, members of the Commission.
Honorable guests.

I am honored to have been invited by your prestigious commission to speak on the theme of "Modern Day Slavery and What We Buy," a subject which is particularly dear to me.

It is thus with great pleasure that I address the Commission, comprised of notable personalities and ardent defenders of equality and human dignity.

This session coincides with a crucial moment in the future of my country, in a context of economic crisis and active denial of the practice of slavery and discrimination.

Please thus allow me to thank you, from the bottom of my heart, for this wonderful opportunity which you have offered me in order to inform you of the daily suffering of slaves and marginalized peoples in Mauritania.

Mr. President, honorable members.

The Mauritanian population, composed of Bambaras, Wolofs, Pulars, Soninkes, Arabo-Berbers and Haratines, currently live in a society characterized by profound disparity and ancient practices, sustained by a system of discriminatory governance and exclusion.

The Haratines, the main victims of slavery constitute nearly 50% of the Mauritanian population. Broadly this population is poor, uneducated and lives in peripheral communities of Mauritania's main cities and in rural zones. Both the descendants of slaves and slaves are abused without mercy and are excluded from the institutionalized economic system.

According to the the Report of the United Nations' Special Rapporteur on contemporary forms of racism, racial discrimination, xenophobia and related intolerance, Mutuma Ruteree, Mutuma Ruteree: "The Haratines [...] constitute the most important ethnic group in Mauritania, and are also the most politically and economically marginalized group, in a society which remains profoundly stratified along ethnicity, ancestry, caste and class. The word *Haratine* is derived from an Arabic word which indicates freedom, which points to the fact that the rest of society considers them as freed slaves."

The same report indicates that "...approximately 50% of the Haratines live in conditions of slavery, submitted to domestic servitude, forced labor or bonded labor. They remain marginalized and underrepresented in political posts and in public service. In 2013, only 5 of 95 seats at the National Assembly were occupied by Haratines and only 1 senator out of 56 belonged to this group. On top of this, only 2 of 13 regional governors and 4 of 53 regional state representatives were Haratine."

"The Haratine make up 80% of the illiterate population with 80% of Haratine not having completed elementary school, and representing only 5% of students at institutions of higher education. More than 90% of the dock workers, domestic workers and workers of low-skilled and low paying jobs are Haratine, whereas only 2% of high-level officials and senior public and private sector leaders derive from this group."

Full power, as well as the economic benefits are controlled by the Arabo-Berber community.

Mr. President, honorable members.

Foremost, I would like to point out the duplicity which the Mauritanian State and the dominant groups use to scoff at international opinion and make light of the country's partners. Indeed, modern anti-slavery and anti-discrimination laws are decreed, a road map deliberately omitting the existence of the scourge has been compiled, the country adheres to the principal international instruments for defending human dignity, but, at the same time, the State continues to protect and extend all the privileges solely to the Arabo-Berber community. The State promotes the models of old, drawn from manuals of pro-slavery exegesis; those writings are explicit generators of race-based inequality. They divide Muslims into masters and slaves and stipulate that the slave is his master's property and that his master can sell him, give him away, use him as security, give him as a gift, etc. The master thus enjoys the labor of his slave without paying him wages and he has access to the bodies of female slaves against their will, no matter how old they are or how many they are. A master can thus use and abuse his female slaves, as he pleases.

This description —not complete — of the Black Code, still in effect and taught in numerous law schools and divinity schools, finds itself codified in the books which we have symbolically burned on April 27, 2012 in Nouakchott.

In Mauritania, in the area of Lebyar (zone of the wells), located in the region of the Hodh El Chargui, not far from the border with Mali, un pro-slavery master today can still castrate his slave if the slave's handsomeness is likely to elicit the desire of noble women.

IRA-Mauritania and SOS-Slaves, one of the principal and officially recognized anti-slavery organizations in Mauritania, continually draws the attention of the authorities, both at the central and local levels, on the gross abuses endured by the slaves, but the elicited responses are still far from what we expect.

Mr. President, honorable members.

As a reminder, in 2013 the country put in place a governmental solidarity agency called TADAMOUN. This agency, meant to support victims of slavery, was voided of all substance. Today this agency is a political propaganda tool, completely guided and controlled by those close to masters and stakeholders in the system of slavery. The actions undertaken by this agency are not for the benefit of the real victims. In reality, all the victims of slavery identified in the regions of Hodhs, Trarza, Assaba, Brakna, Adrar and Nouakchott have never benefited from any assistance from this agency. In these regions, women who have escaped slavery and moved to large urban areas do not receive any governmental assistance. These women are very poor, uneducated, often divorced or never married but have children borne from repeated rape by their former masters. They have to provide for the many needs of their families. This exposes them to a debauched lifestyle where morality is in grave jeopardy.

The programs initiated by this agency are very often put in the hands of Arabo-Berber businessmen who are close to power and who continue to enrich themselves much to the discontentment of the Haratine masses, poor and bound in servitude, who are the very people these programs are supposed to help. The true defenders of the rights of slaves are not asked to be part of the conception or the management, let alone the inaction, of the policies of this anti-slavery commission.

In addition, the State has given this agency the right to bring civil suits in cases of slavery. This is in direct contradiction with principles of victim protection and is devoid of all credibility. Indeed, the State as represented by the prosecutor remains in control by virtue of this government agency and is a party in these slavery-related court cases. The opportunity to be a civil party is a right that civil society has often demanded in vain when pursuing matters of slavery.

Mr. President, honorable members

In December 2013, my country announced the creation of a special court to deal exclusively with slavery and slavery-related crimes, but up until today not one measure has been taken to clarify its composition, its place within the legal framework, its prerogatives and guarantees of its independence.

Mr. President, honorable members

Since the enactment of the law criminalizing slavery in 2007, none of the cases brought before the judiciary have been dealt with appropriately. Take the case of the two brothers Said and Yargue in 2011, for which one sentence was handed down. Today the case is with the criminal division of the Nouakchott court of appeals, due to the liberation of the one convicted person, after only 3 months of detention and the annullment of the sentence.

In Mauritania, household servants constitute an extremely exploited, marginal population that enjoys no legal protections. In 2011, the country enacted a decree regulating domestic labor, but it was not applied and went unheeded.

Cases of human trafficking toward the Gulf countries have been pointed out several times without the State ever taking appropriate protective measures. The victims of this trafficking are generally exploited as household servants or as sex workers.

In 2013, a Mauritanian academic, as a guest on the Suadi Arabian television show *Rissala*, tried to deny the existence of slavery in the country. The show's host informed the academic that he himself was acquainted with people who had received a gift of slaves from Mauritania who were working as household servants.

Our organization is also very concerned with the fate of Zahra, a young girl who has been held for over 17 years in the United Arab Emirates by a family of Mauritanian origin. Despite her mother and sister's pleas, Zahra remains impossible to contact and it appears her employers are using her for household labor and for sex. This case has been extensively documented by our organization.

Mr. President, honorable members

The Mauritanian state has established a patronage system skewed in favor of Arab-Berbers in all sectors of the national economy: mining, fishing, manufacturing, services, etc. This system allocates exclusively to Arab-

Berbers the benefits required for activity in these sectors. They thus are able to amass heaping profits, which allows the domination and exploitation of slaves to continue. Descendants of slaves and Afro-Mauritanians are exploited in these econmic sectors and paid meager salaries.

Mr. President, honorable members

Our organization's anti-slavery activists are regularly arrested, tortured and imprisoned. Today, Hanana Ould MBoïrick and Boubacar Ould Yatma are serving a year in prison without parole, and Cheikh Ould Vall has been handed a six-month prison sentence. These activists were jailed for organizing to defend women who were being dispossessed of their land in the Dar Naim neighborhood of Nouakchott.

I formally demand their unconditional release without delay. I also demand that an investigation be launched into the expropriation of Haratine and Afro-Mauritanian lands. The justice system must identify those responsible and condemn them appropriately.

In addition to the practice of hereditary slavery, the Mauritanian state fosters a system that excludes and discriminates against the Afro-Mauritanian community.

Despite many complaints and denunciations of abuse against blacks between 1989 and 1991, no legal action has been taken against those who were allegedly responsible. Law 92 (1993) granted amnesty to military and security forces personnel who had committed violations during this period. The families of the victims of these abuses are today living with disastrous socioeconomic conditions. 5

Given the enthusiasm of young people for our cause, and in the face of numerous attempts to slander us, we created a committee for peace in 2011. The jailed militants are all members of this committee.

Our commitment to the peaceful exchange of power and to the acknowledgement of the legitimate aspirations of the Haratines and other marginalized communities led us to campaign in the June 2014 presidential election. This experience was a valuable opportunity to raise national and international awareness about the disparities and the suffering of disadvantaged classes in my country.

The economic and media resources mobilized by those in power and the countless privations and threats we were subjected to did not prevent us from taking our message to people all over the country.

The opacity of the electoral system and the many irregularities observed drove us to contest the result and appeal to the constitutional council. Unfortunately, this appeal did not make it to court.

Mr. President, honorable members

People responsible for the crime of slavery are protected by the Mauritanian state and enjoy total immunity. More than 30 cases of slavery, mostly affecting women and children, are pending before national courts, without any convictions handed down. Taking advantage of the fear and ignorance of the slaves, Mauritanian courts of law always use the ruse of paying very small sums of money to victims, disguised as reparations.

Mr. President, honorable members

Victims of slavery and injustice in my country need you to convince Mauritania's government to end the political, economic and diplomatic policies of impoverishing and denying justice to vulnerable populations, by recognizing the existence of the massive-scale slavery to which the Haratines are subjected.

They need you to convince Mauritania to cease its hypocrisy and apply its national laws as well as the international laws that Mauritania has officially adopted.

They need you so that funding from solidarity organization TADAMOUN may end up in the hands of the real victims of slavery and exclusion, not enrich groups corrupt Arabo-Berber businessmen who steal these resources.

We need you to help us abolish the teaching a valorization of slavery and other forms of inequality that are part of our books and age-old codes and that only our country still grants immunity and inviolability today.

To conclude, I would like to pay tribute to all militants, women and men, of IRA and SOS-Esclaves, and to all my friends, and my family, for their sacrifices and loyalty for the cause we defend.

Long live a reconciled Mauritania.

Thank you for your kind attention.

Washington DC, 07/24/2014

Ms. BONAMICI. Thank you very much for that very compelling testimony.

I am going to ask a question to each of you and I will start with the last witness, Mr. Abeid. Thank you very much for that testimony. It was very compelling and, obviously, your country has just recently abolished slavery and criminalized slavery only in 2007.

But, obviously, based on your testimony there is still a lot of work to do. The commission has formed. Nothing has happened. Prosecutions are not moving forward.

So what role can the United States and the international community -- what role can we play to support your efforts? Is your legal infrastructure in place to ensure that your country can effectively combat slavery if there is prosecution and enforcement? So how -- what can we do?

Mr. DAH ABEID. There is everything left to do because the government has yet not done anything actually on the ground. My anti-slavery organization is not legally allowed in Mauritania. The people who -- the militants who are fighting against slavery they are in prison.

They are prohibited from working. They are stopped from working in the country. They cannot even earn a living because you cannot work for -- against slavery and also earn your life.

Though Mauritania has clearly ratified many international instruments against trafficking in persons, against slavery, against discrimination, against trafficking in people and selling people, the U.S. really needs to point to Mauritania and call them out on not complying with the international treaties that it has become party to and the United States can really play a very important role in this because the U.S. is a very, very close partner of Mauritania, the first number-one partner.

Right now, I am here because I am in provisional liberty, me and seven of my friends. Seven of my friends and I actually have cases pending against us in Mauritanian court, which can be handed down at any moment.

So being here is even a provisional liberty due to my fight against slavery. So international treaties and conventions against slavery that Mauritania ratifies is only for external consumption.

It is not for implementation on the ground, and there has not been a single case of a slave owner being actually prosecuted and put in jail.

Ms. BONAMICI. Thank you very much. I know it takes a lot of courage to do what you do in your country. We are fortunate to have you here sharing the importance of the work yet to be done and we look forward to further conversations about what our country and the international community can do.

So thank you again on behalf of the commission. Mr. Eaves, I wanted to ask you -- you talked about what your organization does to educate. What happens when there is a victim of trafficking or forced labor?

What about when they go back home, say, for example, they are helped and assisted by either your organization or another NGO. Do they get any services? What happens when they get back home to their home country? Is there anyone helping them afterward?

Mr. EAVES. We always want to make sure -- that is an excellent question -- we always want to make sure that whenever we see a child or an adult removed from forced labor that they get the full range of services that they deserve.

So that is not just the short-term provision of services immediately after they are removed. But we want to make sure that they make it all the way back to a community, either their home community or any community where they will feel safe and can resume a normal life again.

So in the case of both Min Min and Wolde, once they were removed from the forced labor there was a period where they stayed with a service provider that we partner with. In Wolde's case he stayed directly with World Vision. In Min Min's case, he worked with a partner.

And then we helped trace back where they came from and then worked because in -- with Min Min's case he was going from Indonesia to -- back to Burma. We worked with the

International Organization of Migration to make sure that he made it safely back to Burma and then our staff on the ground in Burma worked with him to get him back to his home community.

They let his community and his parents in particular know that he was alive and then worked with them. There is obviously a long healing process that takes place. When you have been gone for nine years and you have been subjected to the kind of trauma that these children and adults are subjected to, you don't just assert yourself back into normal life overnight.

And so there is intense efforts made to make sure that both the survivor and their family are getting to a point where they are comfortable and they can start living their lives normally again.

And so a lot of work is done to make sure that particularly for the survivor's community that they will be welcomed back, that they will -- there will be an opportunity for them either in education or some sort of employment so that they never have to try to leave to find a job again that could wind up an exploitation.

Ms. BONAMICI. Thank you. I just want to point out that there are certainly challenges when someone has been away for so long and with sext trafficking it is really difficult as well and, you know, a completely different set of issues sometimes. But I know that when we have had conversations here in this country about sex trafficking how the services are provided to the victims so that they do not feel as if they are criminals, and some people want to incarcerate them until they can get services and others feel that that is counterproductive.

But we have to make sure that we have the services in place for those who have been trafficked for labor as well as sex trafficking.

Mr. Viederman, I wanted to follow up on your work that you have done because I was really interested in how you said that you work with client companies and that is typically -- I think that is your approach. It is really, really interesting. You talked about the framework for ethical recruitment.

I wanted to talk about whether the companies that you are working with do more to promote their work and I know the legislation that is pending may address that somewhat. But do they identify their companies as companies that have taken extra steps to assure that they are following laws and labor standards? Do they have a competitive advantage if they do that?

Is there some effort to promote the work because you said it is typically confidential work. How can we build on it, encourage more companies to take that approach of assuring that their products are free from -- in the supply chain from forced labor?

Mr. VIEDERMAN. Thank you. It is a wonderful question. I will repeat that so everyone can hear me. I think it is essential that we bring companies out of the shadows on this issue and that means helping them illuminate in the shadows of their own supply chain so they have a better understanding of what they are doing but then also be willing to stand next to them and say this is a good practice.

There is a very few number -- there is a very small number of companies that are actually doing anything measurable to reduce the vulnerability of people in their supply chains, especially people who are as vulnerable as those who have been trafficked.

But there are a handful and they -- and yet they are still unwilling to stand up and broadcast what they are doing because they are concerned that they -- their consumers will not understand when they talk about forced labor even if they talk about it in the context of doing something good that they will still be somewhat penalized from it.

So I think anything that we can do like this forum, like increased regulation, like opportunities to essentially force companies to start to disclose during which process they will realize the world has not come to an end -- they can still continue to sell their products and indeed probably have benefited substantially by the elimination of unethical middlemen that are in many cases not even known to them, that will help, I think, drag companies out of the shadows on this set of issues.

There are also, however, very few metrics available. So I mentioned one in my remarks, that Apple has facilitated the return of this substantial amount of money.

I sure would love to see a way to highlight other companies doing the same sort of thing. As of yet, that is for me the best indication of a company addressing this issue in a quantitative way that is beneficial to the company and also measurably beneficial to the workers.

So to highlight that somehow and bring that practice into the work of other companies would be a real step forward.

Ms. BONAMICI. And certainly on the flip side there are companies that, I think, their practices have been highlighted and certainly with increased use of social media the consumers of the products, once they find out that there is an issue, for example, with the shrimp in Thailand I think that the consumers can have a significant voice out there in the community and highlighting where they see that there are problems.

But I am trying to find a constructive way to highlight the companies that are stepping up and some states actually have social responsibility corporations. My state of Oregon does. The State of California likely does as well. So we may see this -- hopefully, the companies stepping up and taking steps that they can.

Ms. Misra, I wanted to talk a little bit about labor recruiters. Certainly, there has been an increasing role on the labor recruiters but many of them may be, you know, small operations, particularly hard to monitor.

So how can the United States help ensure that the recruiters are not charging fees for their services, which -- forcing workers into debt bondage for being dishonest about the work? We heard the stories.

In what ways can U.S. companies monitor again to make sure that their workers are not being trafficked or victims of forced labor with particular focus on those recruiters?

Ms. MISRA. Thank you so much for the question, Representative.

Ms. BONAMICI. Is your microphone on?

Ms. MISRA. Yes, it is on. Thank you so much for the question and you actually hit on something that I am very passionate about, and actually World Vision, Verite and the Solidarity Center are all members of a coalition called the Alliance to End Slavery and Trafficking, or ATEST, and we have been working on several years -- for several years on legislation to end fraud in our nonimmigrant visa programs and prevent trafficking through greater regulation of foreign labor recruiters and there is a bill right now pending in the House called H.R. 3344 which is designed to do exactly that.

And to address your question, we think that the best way to be able to address the role that labor recruiters play in increasing the vulnerability in trafficking workers is to ensure first and foremost that they aren't allow to charge fees, and we think that, while it is difficult, as you mentioned, when, you know, labor recruiters have huge networks that go down to maybe just an individual agent in a village it is very difficult to monitor that, we do think that starting with this legislation, H.R. 3344, is a great step forward and we hope it will serve as a model for the rest of the world and for other countries to pass similar legislation because you would be shocked, I think, to see how little regulation there is of labor recruiters around the world.

And so by just having a policy that says you cannot charge fees we think is the first step. The second step in that would be employers. The way that they can monitor this is, one, that they should be required to use a licensed or registered labor recruiter and that is something that this bill is requiring.

You know, the bill provides a safe harbor for employers if they use a registered labor recruiter. But the bill also provides mechanisms for access to justice. So if it is violated and workers are charged a fee, they will now have ways through this bill -- administrative, civil and criminal remedies -- that they could use and access to justice they can use to hold these labor recruiters accountable and they will now know who they are.

Part of the problem is a lot of workers in countries of origin don't even know who the labor recruiter is that the employer hired because of the agents and et cetera that they use below that.

They are often not given full information about the type of visa that they are coming to the United States to work on, et cetera. And so we think that requiring full disclosure, requiring the elimination of fees and registering labor recruiters is a great step forward.

Ms. BONAMICI. Thank you very much.

Mr. Lowenthal, and before I turn it over to Mr. Lowenthal I just want to apologize in advance that I may need to leave before his questioning. But I wanted to thank all of you, each of our witnesses, for your expertise, for helping us on the commission highlight the importance of this issue and for also giving us some good information about the concrete steps that we can take to help address international human trafficking and forced labor. So thank you for being here. Thank you for bringing your expertise. Mr. Lowenthal.

Mr. LOWENTHAL. Thank you. I am going to be brief also because I will have to leave really soon. I want to follow up -- and I want to thank the panel for both your work and what you have done and your educating me and others and also the courage that you have displayed.

I want to follow up on an issue that was raised by the chair talking about what states have done. Now we are looking at federal legislation. My state, for example, has done the California Transparency in Supply Chains, which requires both the retail sellers and the manufacturers who make more than a certain amount of money -- I believe it is $100 million -- in doing business in California to disclose their efforts to eradicate slavery and human trafficking from their direct supply chain.

My issue is as we move forward now we know, and I have heard how difficult it is in the issue around enforcement, how effective -- now, and I believe this bill is now four years. I was a supporter of the bill when I was in the state legislature.

What do we learn from that and that we can modify now as we move forward? I know there are some companies that have done a very good job in trying to comply and there are others that have not. I know that too.

So what have we learned that can really help us as we move forward?

Ms. MISRA. Thank you so much for that question, Representative Lowenthal. Before I address the transparency law, I just want to mention that California also has a bill pending right now on regulating foreign labor recruiters.

Mr. LOWENTHAL. Labor recruiters.

Ms. MISRA. And any support that you could give and speaking to the governor about signing that bill into law once we get it passed. We would really appreciate that because it is in a very crucial stage right now.

Mr. LOWENTHAL. Thank you. I will do that.

Ms. MISRA. So if you could put a little plug in for that.

Mr. LOWENTHAL. A big plug.

Ms. MISRA. And in terms of the California law and transparency, first of all, we were all, again, the Alliance to End Slavery Trafficking that we are members of pushed really hard for that legislation and we are very thankful to California taking the lead in that so that we can use it as a model for the federal legislation.

We have been encountering problems and one of the things that ATEST has been doing has been engaging with the state government to try to get them to release the information about which companies are complying and which companies are not complying, and that would be really helpful for us as advocates and as activists on this issue to be able to have that information.

So again, anything you can do to help that process along would be greatly appreciated. And, unfortunately -- I am going to turn it over to both Jesse and Dan because they can get a little bit more specific -- but we haven't seen as many companies complying as we would like to see and not providing as much specific information as we think would be useful.

A lot of companies have actually just said we are not doing anything and that is the reporting that they put up there, or just providing very limited information. But I will turn it over to these guys for more specifics.

Mr. EAVES. Yes. So what I would say is as we look forward there are a couple of key opportunities coming up in which the U.S. can really assert its leadership role.

So I think what we have learned is that there is a real need to create the incentive and foster, you know, basically the way business works. We want to make sure the companies are rewarded for trying to do the right thing.

No company will be perfect but I think that just making the effort and really -- once you start taking those key steps -- and Verite's research has really fleshed this out over the years -- when you start taking those steps and you start seeing what goes into your supply chain you often find several areas not even related to forced labor and exploitation where you can actually save money.

And so there is often a fear of spending too much up front and that it could cost companies extra. But there are, as we look at what the role the U.S. government plays, and Ambassador CdeBaca mentioned, you know, we are the largest -- the U.S. government is the single largest purchaser in the world, and coming up later this year the G-20 will be meeting in Australia and one of the issues on the table is about a -- they are calling it a common approach to public procurement.

Basically, the G-20 countries all adopting a set of rules and regulations that anyone who wants to sell to them has to follow so that -- and companies like this because they only now will have one set of rules to comply with as opposed to 20 or 100 or however it may be.

And so that is a real key moment for the U.S. to show leadership, to show what we have done already with the executive orders and to maybe push ourselves even further on the issues of, for instance, closing the consumptive demand loophole.

But there are two opportunities -- one, the labor ministers of the G-20 countries are meeting in September in Australia. That is a chance -- you know, the U.S. Department of Labor has done a good job of highlighting best practices in addressing supply chain transparency. And then there is the actual G-20 meeting in November also in Australia where, again, this issue will come up and it is an opportunity for the U.S. to really exert its influence and it is, you know, something that companies we have talked to and have worked with are fond of because they say look, if we only have to follow set of rules and we are going to get rewarded by getting government procurement contracts we are on board. And so those are two opportunities where we can really seize the moment.

Mr. VIEDERMAN. Add a couple of points. First of all, the focus on recruiters is the next -- is the next step. The California act as it stands now requires a company to disclose.

It seems to be acceptable so far to disclose that you are doing nothing or don't really care about the issue. That is a penalty that perhaps there is some legal costs to but there should be more social cost and consumer cost but that is a process that takes -- you know, needs those of us in the activist world and advocate world to sort of take up.

But refining either through the currently California act or in its federal sibling or through the recruitment-specific bill to make sure that the focus is on the increased transparency and requirement of regulating recruiters.

For the vast majority of multinationals at the highest sort of their direct supplier level it is recruitment-driven forced labor that they should be paying attention to. So anywhere there is a presence of third parties, recruiters, warehousing cleaning crews, people who are being essentially given jobs in their general operations without them knowing where it is, that work is being facilitated by these recruiters.

Those companies -- it is going to be harder for them to figure out to what extent they are exposed to a raw material somewhere else. It ought to be very much placed on their table right in front of their CEO's daily priority list that this is something they need to look at at the top level.

So focusing on recruiters and then adding some cost, however that should emerge. I am not a lawyer. I don't know to what extent that is possible but to the extent that this law then gets taken the next step and becomes enforceable so much the better.

Mr. LOWENTHAL. I have some other questions but I am going to submit them in writing. I would like to know what, as the bills in California about recruitment, if you could just speak to my staff so that we can help and kind of -- is that -- do you know it that is with the governor now or is it still in the legislature?

Ms. MISRA. It is still in the legislature. It just passed through one of the committees and I am sorry -- Jesse, do you remember?

Mr. LOWENTHAL. It is okay. Whatever it is, you don't have to get -- just get me all that information. I am really hearing very clearly the point on recruitment now and recruiters. That is really the next step that we have to do and maybe that is something that I can really help on with and I would like to do that.

Ms. MISRA. Thank you so much.

Mr. LOWENTHAL. And I am not going to ask another question but I am, as a psychologist, very much interested in mental health issues and especially and I am going to ask you to maybe help me on that as we move forward also.

But I want to thank the panelists for a wonderful presentation today, great education, and I think this is exactly what the Tom Lantos Human Rights Commission should be doing -- having that forum, educating us and thank you very much.

[Whereupon, at 11:42 a.m., the committee was adjourned.]

Tom Lantos Human Rights Commission Hearing

<u>Modern Day Slavery and What We Buy</u>

Thursday, July 24, 2014
10:00 AM-12:00 PM
2255 Rayburn HOB

Please join the Tom Lantos Human Rights Commission for a hearing on how slavery exists today and how it impacts the production, handling, and distribution of various goods (the global supply chain).

According to a new report by the International Labor Organization (ILO), forced trafficking generates $150 billion in illegal profits per year. Approximately two thirds of the total ($99 billion) is generated from sexual exploitation with approximately $51 billion generated from forced labor.

Trafficking for the purpose of sexual exploitation has historically been the most commonly reported—and prosecuted—form of human trafficking globally. However, victims of forced labor and debt bondage are held in conditions of slavery in a variety of jobs, including agricultural and construction work, domestic servitude and other labor-intensive jobs.

With nearly 30 million people in situations of forced labor and trafficking (according to the 2013 Global Slavery Index), join us as we hear from experts on how this affects the global supply chain and labor market and what our government and organizations are doing to combat the human rights atrocities of modern day slavery.

<u>Panelists</u>
- Amb. Luis CdeBaca, Ambassador-at-Large, Office to Monitor and Combat Trafficking in Persons, Department of State

- Neha Misra, Senior Specialist, Migration and Human Trafficking, Solidarity Center
- Dan Viederman, CEO, Verité
- Jesse Eaves, Senior Policy Advisor For Child Protection, World Vision
- Biram Dah Abeid, Founder, Initiative for the Resurgence of the Abolitionist Movement in Mauritania

For any questions, please contact the Tom Lantos Human Rights Commission at 202-225-3599 or tlhrc@mail.house.gov.

Sincerely,

James P. McGovern
Co-Chair, TLHRC

Frank R. Wolf
Co-Chair, TLHRC